THE
PROPHET OF MODERN INDIA

...equality — ... in all beings, ... this is the
sign of the free

Vivekananda

THE PROPHET OF MODERN INDIA

A Biography of

Swami Vivekananda

GAUTAM GHOSH

Rupa & Co

Published by
Rupa & Co
7/16, Ansari Road, Daryaganj
New Delhi-110 002

Sales Centres:
Allahabad Bangalore Chandigarh Chennai
Hyderabad Jaipur Kathmandu
Kolkata Mumbai Pune

Photographs courtesy: The Ramakrishna Mission Institute of
Culture and the Advaita Ashram.

Book designed & typeset by
Arrt Creations
45 Nehru Apts, Kalkaji
New Delhi - 110 019

Printed in India by
Ajanta Offset & Packagings Ltd.
New Delhi - 110 002

To my late father
who was a devout believer of Sri Ramakrishna,
an ardent devotee of *Maa Kali*,
and was as upright as Swamiji,
although bogged down by the pressures and compromises
of a householder's life.

শ্রীশ্রীরামকৃষ্ণ
শরণম্‌

It was towards the beginning of this year that my friend Barnali came to me one day with a proposal to write some biographies for Rupa, the foremost indigenous publisher of English books in India. I had just about finished editing another author's biographical work of a well known santoor maestro then, and to be honest, I was looking out for such an opportunity with a reputed publisher. Nevertheless, I asked my friend, who has known my flair for writing for sometime now, whether she thought that I could do justice to the great personalities about whose lives she wanted me to write on. The answer being in the affirmative, I was emboldened to dip the feather in ink, and that is the beginning of this episode of my career.

The first biography was for a 'pocket book' biographical series (*Charitavali*) of the publisher. The one on Swamiji was also projected for the same readership. But, as I traversed the vastness of the personality and his work, I found the unfolding of a versatility that is best expressed by another great patriot of our country, Netaji Subhas Chandra Bose, who wrote about Swami Vivekananda, 'I cannot write about Vivekananda without going into raptures. Few indeed could comprehend or fathom him even among those who had the privilege of becoming intimate with him. His personality was rich, profound and complex ... Reckless in his

sacrifice, unceasing in his activity, boundless in his love, profound and versatile in his wisdom, exuberant in his emotions, merciless in his attacks but yet simple as a child, he was a rare personality in this world of ours', and I wondered how I could do justice to such a personality in ten thousand words, the margin set for the *Charitavali* Series.

Moreover, my research on this great life also proved to be an eye-opener for the Bengali chauvinist in me finding out the true Indianness of Swami Vivekananda, who was rather recognised thus by the South and parts of North India long before the Bengalis realised the true potential of their beloved Narendra Nath Dutta. I also found the contemporary relevance of Swamiji's teachings in India in the light of the all prevailing fanaticism and conversions cutting across all religions, and the rising intolerance of the so-called practitioners of that great, all encompassing religion — Hinduism. Swamiji's relevance in today's world — vis-à-vis the turmoil in Kashmir, the USA once again assuming the role of the sole superpower and searching out excuses to declare war on countries which are already in physical and emotional ruins, the Church perceiving *yoga* as a threat to it, and such other forms of intolerance — is becoming more profound. I therefore requested the publisher to give me an opportunity to sketch a biography that will help the reader get the right perspective of one of the greatest thinkers of all times, and I have to admit that the publisher was magnanimous enough to give a one-book-author like me a free hand to write. I honestly believe that I have not let them down on this account, although, being the novice that I am, and not yet having mastered the art of churning novels by the dozens, I have missed a host of deadlines mutually set by the publisher in tandem with me.

Writing about this 'Prince among men, a man in a million' was a pleasant but heady experience, and I often had to cut out myself from my work to let the matter sink in before being able to write on it. His knowledge was not only 'profound and versatile' but expansive as well. I would not know the virtue of *brahmacharya* that Swamiji so vehemently prescribed for his disciples, and will never be able to comprehend his proclamation that its practice in strictness bestowed on one a unique memory whereby one could remember anything by just reading it, or even hearing it, only once; but the depth of Swamiji's knowledge in virtually anything and everything, and his ability to speak extempore on any subject any where in just those thirty-nine years of his short life, make me wonder as to why no other *bhramachari,* even from the Order of Monks that he established, could reach anywhere near him! A journey through his life is a study of not only the ethos of India and the *Sanatana Dharma,* but also a lucid lesson in the history, geography and civilisation of any and all countries, nay cities, that he travelled through as a *parivrajaka* for twelve years.

In this endeavour to portray a true picture of the great soul, I have studied the two volume *The Life of Swami Vivekananda* and the nine volume *The Complete Works of Swami Vivekananda,* as published by the Advaita Ashram, in quite some depth, and also browsed through many of the numerous websites giving varied information on Swamiji. I am indebted to all of them for the little knowledge that I could assimilate from their vast ventures. I had also taken the opportunity of visiting Varanasi and Sarnath recently to do some more research on Swamiji, and am obliged to *Brahmachari* Prabir Maharaj of the Ramkrishna Mission Home of Service, Varanasi, for his spontaneous help in trying to find out about 'Gopallal Villa', where Swamiji had stayed during his last visit to Varanasi exactly a hundred years ago, in 1902, and Ven. Kahawatte Siri Sumedha Thero, the High Priest of the Mulagandhakuty Vihara and *Bhikkhu*-in-charge of the Sarnath Centre of Maha Bodhi Society of India for throwing new light on Swamiji's relationship with Dharmapala. I am thankful to Tarun Maharaj of the Ramakrishna Mission Institute of Culture and Arabinda Maharaj of Advaita Ashrama, Kolkata, for their kind help and guidance in acquiring the photographs of Swami Vivekananda.

The reader will sadly find that Swamiji's distress at the degradation of the glorious ancient culture of the country by the stupid activities and dichotomous lives of its so-called leaders, who preached reforms but did not practise it, as being true even today, as is his observation, 'Three men cannot act in concert together in India for five minutes. Each one struggles for power, and in the long run the whole organisation (read country) comes to grief.' Swamiji's description of the importance of India in the world civilisation is as lucid as his observations on the development of the Suez Canal and the ports around it. His remarks on conversion of the low, the poor and the miserable — 'Don't think that it is merely the pinch of hunger that drives them to Christianity. It is simply because they do not get your sympathy' — should make today's leaders try and rectify the situation.

Swamiji reminds those who wear the *gerua* that, 'the *gerua* is not for enjoyment, rather it is the banner for heroic work.' He proclaimed his mission to create an Order of monks in India who would dedicate their lives for others, improve the living condition of the masses through their service, and bring about a religious renewal by spreading the teachings of the Master, which included the establishment of fellowships amongst followers of different religions. He was also quick to realise that in India one had to reach out to the masses and not wait for the multitudes to come, and thus advised his followers to go 'from door to door' to preach the 'truths as preached and practised by Sri Ramakrishna and to help others to put these truths into practice.' Although he did stress on the observation of strict discipline and regulations by the *brahmacharis,* he would say that 'our main object is to transcend all rules and regulations', and had himself protested against the elaborate paraphernalia of daily worship in the *Math.* I am sure that there is scope for introspection by the Ramakrishna Mission authorities as to their success to date in spreading this mission of their founder, and to what role they can play in bringing about a religious harmony in India today.

I have strived to spell the Indian words and names phonetically as they are supposed to be pronounced, and have also included a glossary of the Indian terms used in the book towards the end. The details of some of Swamiji's lectures have been included so that the diligent reader can make further readings of these, most of which are available as individual booklets.

I am thankful to my publishers for bearing with me through this lengthy venture in time. I am also thankful to my wife and son who have stood by me through all these months, often sacrificing their wishes and the necessities of my company, and also to those relations I have acquired in my life for excusing me for not being by them as often as I used to be earlier.

Kolkata
Gautam Ghosh
12 December 2002

one

The Birth of the Wanderer

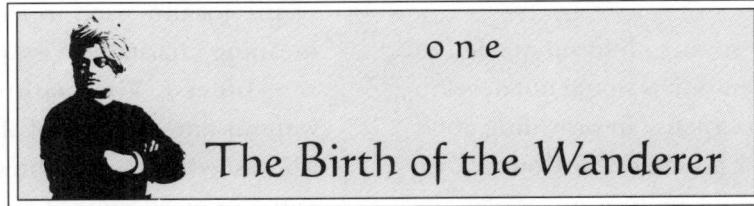

Swami Vivekananda's original name was Narendranath Dutta, and his ancestral house was on Gour Mohan Mukherjee Lane, Simla Street — a north Calcutta locality. His great grandfather Ram Mohan Dutta was the associate of an English solicitor, and had amassed a huge fortune through his profession. He had a large family, was rich and powerful, and was renowned as a man with sound learning, strong independent spirit and charitable leanings.

Ram Mohan Dutta had two sons, Durgaprasad and Kaliprasad. Durgaprasad was well-versed in Persian and Sanskrit, and was skilled in law. He became a partner of his father in his law firm, but had a strong penchant for a monastic life. He renounced the world in 1835 when he was just twenty-five years of age, and became a monk. He had one son named Viswanath who was brought up by his mother Shyamasundari, a devout but fearless woman.

After Durgaprasad renounced the world, Viswanath's uncle Kaliprasad became the head of the family. However, Kaliprasad had no source of income and hence the accumulated wealth of the family started dwindling. As ill luck would have it,

Viswanath's mother passed away when he was only ten years old. Viswanath became an orphan, and was cheated by his uncle at every step. In spite of the sorry situation that he was in, Viswanath carried on the family tradition of learning, and became proficient in several languages. He mastered Bengali, English, Persian, Arabic, Urdu, Hindi and of course, Sanskrit. Like his father, Viswanath also had a sweet voice and at one time, took music lessons too. Although history was his forte, he also acquired a good knowledge of astrology and later on, cast the horoscopes of his own children.

After completing his education, Viswanath first tried his hand at business, but was not successful. He then began apprenticeship under a British attorney by the name of Temple, and after qualifying as an attorney in 1866, he set up practice in partnership with Ashutosh Dhar. After some time, he settled in the legal profession independently and was enrolled as an attorney-at-law in the Calcutta High Court.

As an attorney, Viswanath made considerable reputation for himself, and his area of work spread over the whole of northern India. As he earned a great deal through his profession, he enjoyed a luxurious life, surrounded by friends and relatives and attended by servants. He was a connoisseur of good cooking, and was himself an expert in the art.

He believed that growing children needed to eat well, as otherwise their brains would not develop properly. He spared no expense in providing good and nourishing food for his children. However, he did not believe in leaving behind an enormous patrimony, but rather stressed on a high standard of living and good education, and health for his children, which would then prepare them to make suitable arrangements for their own future. He had observed his uncle Kaliprasad, son of an affluent father who did nothing but spend the inherited wealth, and compared it with his own life of starting off as a poor orphan and becoming wealthy through his own efforts.

Apart from his intellectual attainments, Viswanath was endowed with many good qualities that endeared him to all. He was independent in spirit, generous in disposition, devoted to his friends and a protector of the needy. He would be overcome at the sight of anyone in distress, and would help him unstintingly. Many students — who were distant relatives — used to stay at his house and receive good education at his expense. People of the locality used to call him '*data* Viswanath', meaning charitable Viswanath.

Indeed, Viswanath spent his ample means without any thought of the morrow, giving to all who asked. He even showed a lack of discretion, and supported some of his relatives who languished in idleness, even in drunkenness. While one of his sons criticised his charity as a disease, his eldest son Naren was also against bestowing charity upon worthless persons; but Viswanath would say, 'How can you understand the great miseries of life? When you realize it, you will sympathise with the poor creatures, who try to forget their sorrows in the momentary oblivion obtained through intoxicants.'

Viswanath maintained a broad outlook and possessed vast knowledge cutting across different aspects of life. A liberal Hindu with a receptive mind, he desired to know the essential and universal teachings of all religions. He studied both the Bible and the Dewan-i-Hafiz. He had progressive views and wrote a book in 1882 which mentioned about the harmful superstitions he came across during his travels in northern and central India. Viswanath also defended the remarriage of widows, championed by Ishwar Chandra Vidyasagar, another social stalwart of the time.

Those times were a transitional period in India's history. The new civilisation that had grown through the intermingling of Hindu and Islamic cultures was still prevalent, but European culture had also begun to make its presence felt on Indian life. The educated Indians of the time naturally came under all these three influences, and

Bhuvaneshwari Devi (1841-1911).

(opp.) Vivekananda's ancestral house (foreground) at 3 Gour Mohan Mukherjee Lane, Calcutta.

Viswanath was no exception. His conduct was marked by Hindu-Islamic culture on the one hand, and European influence on the other, and both Brahmins and Muslim *fakirs* received alms and sympathy from him. However, he did not endeavour to make any change in the traditional ways of religious practice in his family.

In 1851, when Viswanath was sixteen, he was married to the ten-year-old Bhuvaneswari Devi, the only child of Nandalal Basu of the renowned Basu family of Simla, Calcutta. Being the only child of her parents, she inherited her paternal property, which later on accrued to her children. As she grew older, Bhuvaneswari Devi became an expert in the management of the household and cheerfully shouldered the responsibility of her husband's large family. She was exceptionally intelligent and found time — even in the midst of many chores — for sewing, music, and the daily study of the Ramayana and the Mahabharata. Graceful, devoted, and full of the fire of one born to regality, she commanded the respect and veneration of all who came in contact with her. She was deeply religious, and worshipped Shiva daily. Calm and resigned to the will of God in all circumstances, this noble Hindu woman always lent a helping hand to all those who needed it.

It was to these two — Viswanath and Bhuvaneswari Devi — that the boy Naren, or 'Bilay' as he was fondly called, and who later became Swami Vivekananda, the greatest man of his age and one who laid the foundation of a new order, was born.

Bhuvaneswari Devi was blessed with motherhood at an early age, but both her first child, a son, and her second, a daughter, died in their childhood. The next three children were all daughters — Haramohini, Swarnamoyee, and another who also died in childhood. So she longed for a son who would carry on the family name and be the link between the past and the future. For hundreds of years, Hindu women have always placed their wants and complaints before the household deity, and have practiced various austerities while waiting to receive the blessings of the Lord. Bhuvaneshwari also prayed to her household deity that her desire might be fulfilled. It has also been the custom, for one in dire need, or anxious that some special event should occur, to make offerings and sacrifices to Lord Shiva at Varanasi. And those who lived far away from that holy city would usually make their offerings through a relative or friend residing there. Bhuvaneshwari Devi wrote to an old aunt of the Dutta family in Varanasi, requesting her to make the necessary offerings and prayers to Lord Vireshwar, the Shiva of the brave heart — situated in the Siddha Kshetra just above the Scindia Ghat — who is specially propitiated when praying for a son. An arrangement was made with the aunt to worship the Vireshwar Shiva at Varanasi every Monday, while Bhuvaneshwari would practise special austerities on every monday in Calcutta. It was believed that if a

woman observed a vow of this sort for one year, she would be blessed with a son. Thus, having complete faith that her prayers would be answered, Bhuvaneshwari waited for one year. She spent her days in practising *japa* and meditation and observed fasts and intensified her other austerities. Her whole soul was immersed in intense faith, and her heart, in the love of Lord Shiva. She would mentally traverse to Varanasi, uniting in thought with the venerable aunt as she poured the sacred Ganga water on the *Shiva-lingam*, or worshipped Him with flowers and mantras. One night, Bhuvaneshwari had a vivid dream wherein she saw the Lord Shiva rouse Himself from His meditation and take the form of a small child who was to be born to her as a son. She woke up and a joyous prayer welled up from her heart. She was now confident that the long months of supplication were over and that the vision was an announcement that her prayers were to be answered.

Her prayers were finally answered on Monday, 12th January 1863 when a son was truly born to her.

It was the *brahma-muhurt*, exactly 33 minutes and 33 seconds after six, a few minutes before sunrise. At the time of birth, the constellation Sagittarius was rising in the east, the moon was in the constellation Virgo, the planet Jupiter was in the eleventh house, and Saturn was in the tenth from that of his birth. It was the seventh day of the ninth Bengali month *Poush*, and happened to be the day of the *Makara Sankranti*, a great Hindu festival. Little did the millions of men and women, observing the festival across the country, know that they had just welcomed the birth of one who was to usher in a new age of glory for the country, reorganize the spiritual and national consciousness of India, and become a great apostle — a St. Paul preaching unto the world another gospel of redemption, namely the message of *Vedanta*. And only a few miles north of Calcutta, in the garden of Dakshineswar, a great saint was waiting for the coming of this baby, who was destined to spread his message and carry on his great work.

The Dakshineswar Temple (founded 1855): Sri Ramakrishna lived and taught here.

Swami Vivekananda

The members of the Dutta family were surprised to see the features of the newborn child. They resembled in many ways those of his grandfather — Durgaprasad — who had renounced the world and they wondered if the monk had been reborn. Thus, there was a lot of pondering as to the naming of the infant, and while some suggested naming him Durgaprasad, the mother suggested that he be named Vireshwar, whose boon he was. Everyone agreed to this, and so they started calling him 'Bilay' for short. Later, his family name became Narendranath, and he was often addressed as Naren.

As a child, Narendranath was naughty. Bribes and threats did not work on him. Finally, Bhuvaneshari discovered that pouring cold water on his head and simultaneously chanting the name of Shiva did quieten him, and so did threats like 'Shiva will not let you go to Kailash if you do not behave'. And soon after Bilay would become his eager, joyous self again. It was such tantrums that prompted the mother to say, 'I prayed to Shiva for a son and He sent me one of His demons!'

These outbursts apart, Naren was a bright, sweet and loving child, and would scamper to anyone who would take him on the lap. He was one of those children who trust all implicitly, and feel joy each moment of that period when the world is a constant surprise. Naren teased his two elder sisters a lot, and they were no match for him. He had a number of pets with which he loved playing, and was especially fond of the family cow, which was venerated by his sisters as *Bhagwati* or cow-mother. Of the servants, he considered the coachman as his friend and idol; the syce, with his grand turban, splendid livery and stately whip, was someone who captured the young child's imagination completely.

Naren had a great fancy for wandering monks, and whenever a *sadhu* or a holy man would approach the Duttas' door, he would rush towards him with all glee. One day, a monk came and asked for alms. All that Naren had on him was a hand-embroidered dhoti around his waist. He was fond of the dhoti, for it was the first garment pronouncing his crossing over from infancy to childhood, but he had no qualms in giving it to the *sadhu*, who tied it around his head and left, blessing the boy. Naren's father, Viswanath Dutta had the memory of his father becoming a monk — and although he himself was very hospitable to *sadhus* — after this incident started keeping a close guard on Naren. Naren was locked up whenever any *sadhu* came, and was freed only after the wanderer left. But this too failed to disconcert the child, and he would throw from the window to the caller anything that he could lay his hands on.

The mother's lap is the first school of any child, and Bhuvaneswari was eager to educate her child well. Naren became aware of the glory of the Hindu gods and goddesses and the greatness of the Indian sages, and learnt about his ancestors. He enhanced the spiritual sense of the listener.

His mother initiated him to the Bengali alphabet, and also to the First Book of English by Pyaricharan Sarkar. It was from his mother again that he learned how to hold aloft his moral standards even while struggling with the vagaries of the world, and how to take refuge at the feet of God who was the best support in life. His mother would tell him: 'Remain pure all your life; guard your own honour and never transgress the honour of others; be tranquil but, when necessary, harden your heart.'

also heard the tales of the Indian epics. Naren would sit quietly through the daily afternoon readings of the Ramayana and the Mahabharata, and listen with rapt attention. He also learnt many things from his maternal grandmother, and her mother, who belonged to the *Vaishnav* sect and knew many teachings and anecdotes from the *Bhagavad Gita* and the *Vaishnav* lore. Many street singers thronged the Duttas' residence, and Naren's mother would welcome them so that Naren could be exposed to the joyous singing of the Lord or the sacred stories put into songs. Beggars they might be, but Bhuvaneswari was aware of the influence they possessed in their ecstatic renderings which

Throughout his life Narendranath loved his mother with all his heart, and used to say, 'He who cannot literally worship his mother can never become great,' and on many an occasion he proudly declared, 'I am indebted to my mother for the efflorescence of my knowledge.'

Other members of the household also contributed to Naren's education. An old relative, Nrisimha Dutta was very learned in Sanskrit lore, and taught Naren the finer points of the Sanskrit grammar *Mugdhabodha*, the genealogy of his family, hymns to gods and goddesses, as well as passages of great length from the Ramayana and Mahabharata.

Naren's father also played a significant role in his education. It was he who insisted that Naren study music — a source of much innocent joy. Perhaps this early grounding helped Narendranath become an accomplished singer later in life.

The first seed of spiritual life was sown during this period of Naren's early education. He had listened enraptured to readings from the Ramayana, and had followed the long story of Rama's struggle and conquest, with all the thrill of enjoying a personal romantic adventure. At these readings, he observed the elder members of the family sitting in worship and meditation, and it occurred to him that he too should worship Rama. One day, he and a little Brahmin boy named Hari purchased a clay image of Sita-Rama, and when no one was about, they climbed the stairs that led to a room on the roof above the women's quarters. After securely closing the door, they installed the image, and sat down to meditate. Meanwhile, parents of both the boys noticed their prolonged absence, and there was an anxious search for them. The hunt led at last to the little locked room on the roof. The searchers knocked and shouted, but there was no response. At last their strong blows broke the latch, and the door flew open. Hari, his meditation disturbed at the first ominous signal, had fled down the stairs. But Naren had not heard anything. He was seated before the flower-decked image, motionless and in deep meditation. When he did not respond on being called by name, he was shaken out of his meditation; but he insisted on being left alone. So, although it seemed strange for his age, but not knowing what to deduce from it, they let him remain there.

Shortly after this, the all-knowing syce created a disturbance in Naren's immature mind. One day when the boy was visiting the stable, the talk drifted to marriage, and the syce, with the bitter memory of some personal experience, forcefully denounced marriage, drawing a dreadful picture of married life. But Rama and Sita were also married! This brought about an irreconcilable conflict between the words of the syce and Naren's regard for the image of Sita-Rama, and caused deep anguish in his heart. He burst into tears as one of the golden dreams of his childhood was broken. Naren ran to the women's quarters. His mother saw his tears and inquired what made him sad. First there was silence, and then sobbing aloud he asked, 'How can I worship Sita-Rama? Was not Sita Rama's wife?' he asked. Intuitively, Bhuvaneshari understood the anguish of her son, but was at a loss as to how to console him? Then, like a flash of lightning in the dark, the thought of Shiva came to her mind. She then addressed her son not as Naren but as

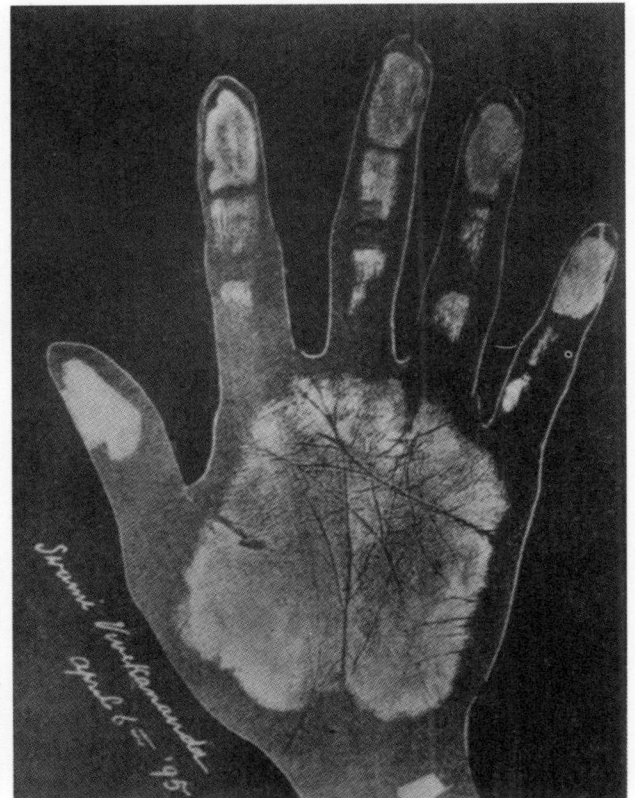

Vireshwar, and said, 'There is Shiva to worship!' These words settled deeply in Naren's heart. Shortly afterwards, Naren left the room and, unseen in the gloom of the evening, climbed the stairs to the roof and opened the door of the room where he had installed the image of Sita-Rama. He paused for a moment, then clasped the image and went to the edge of the roof. The next moment, he threw it down and the image of Sita-Rama was smashed on the pavement below. On the following day Naren bought an image of Shiva with the money given by his mother and placed it where Rama and Sita had been dethroned. Soon, he was found seated before Shiva, with eyes closed to all outer things, and in deep meditation.

Nevertheless, his devotion to Sita-Rama was never destroyed, and, all through his childhood, he had a great fascination for the Ramayana. He was present at all the Ramayana readings in the neighbourhood, and would raptly listen to all the thrilling episodes of Rama's life. Hanuman, the matchless devotee of Lord Rama, particularly enthralled him. But it was Shiva, the god of renunciation, whom he now worshipped.

Even in childhood he fancied becoming a *sanyasi*, a monk. One day he was found moving about nude except for an ochre loincloth, just like the *sadhus* wrapped around themselves. His mother was alarmed to see him thus, and inquired, 'Why Naren, what are you up to?' Naren replied, 'I am Shiva! Look, I am Shiva!' The elders of the household had once jokingly told him that if one meditated, one's hair would become as long and matted as the monks', and these locks would gradually penetrate deep into the earth like the roots of a banyan tree. So the simple child, seated in meditation, would once in a while open his eyes to see if his hair had grown long and matted. But when his expectations were not fulfilled, he ran in bewilderment to his mother, and asked, 'I have meditated, but why has no matted hair grown?' His mother consoled him, 'It is not grown in an hour or a day. It takes many many days, yes, many many months, before matted locks can be grown.' To a child born in a Hindu household reincarnation is an accepted fact, albeit unconsciously, so he added, 'I think I have been a *sadhu* once. Will Shiva let me go to Him if I am good?' The mother answered, 'Yes.' But her heart sank at the thought that perhaps he, too, like his grandfather, would renounce the world and go to Shiva. Then she banished the thought, thinking that there were many years yet before he could grow old enough to take such a decision.

Narendra in meditation.

(opp.) Sri Ramakrishna.

From this time onwards, little Naren would often play his game of meditation, which, nevertheless awakened deep spiritual emotions in him. He would be seen sitting quietly all by himself for a long time, introspecting and detached from all that was happening around him. So deep was this contemplation that sometimes he had to be shaken from it to make him return to the normal condition of a child. Over the period of time, it grew more and more difficult to rouse him on such occasions. The boys of the neighbourhood sometimes joined him in this pastime.

One evening, when the crescent moon was in the sky and they had seated themselves in meditation in the worship-hall, one of the boys noticed a big cobra gliding along the stone paved floor. He shouted out, and while the others sprang to their feet in terror, Naren remained lost in meditation. His friends shouted to him, but there was no response. They ran to his parents, who came in haste. They were absolutely horrified to see a cobra in front of Naren, poised with its hood spread, as if strangely fascinated! They were afraid to call out lest they disturb the snake and provoke it to strike. Then suddenly it went away, and a moment later it was nowhere to be found. When his parents inquired why he did not run away, Naren said, 'I knew nothing of the snake or of anything else; I was feeling inexpressible bliss.'

Every night, before he drifted off to sleep, Naren had the same strange vision. As soon as he lay on the bed and closed his eyes, he would visualise a wonderful spot of light between his eyebrows, and would experience the spot changing hues and expanding, bursting and bathing his whole body in a flood of white radiance. As his mind became preoccupied with this phenomenon, his body would fall asleep. It was a daily occurrence, and he thought that such a phenomenon was a perfectly natural thing which happened to everybody, so he did not mention it until long after. Once he asked a schoolmate, 'Do you see a light

between your eyebrows at night when you go to sleep?' The friend said he did not. 'I do', said Naren, 'Try to remember. Do not fall off to sleep as soon as you go to bed and be on the alert for a while and you will see it.'

In later years, there was to be someone who would put that very question to Naren himself: 'Naren, my boy, do you see a light when you go to sleep?' This questioner was his spiritual teacher, Sri Ramakrishna. The phenomenon remained with him till the end, although in the latter part of his life it was not so frequent or so intense. Such a happening definitely spoke of a great spiritual past in which the soul had learnt to sink itself deep in meditation so well that the meditative state had become spontaneous with it.

three

Laying the Foundation

At the age of six, Naren joined a *pathshala*, the traditional Indian primary school. It was his first day, and he was wearing a brand-new dhoti and carrying a mat under his arm. From his waist dangled a little reed-pen attached to a long string. It was indeed an important day for him. Early in the morning, the family priest conducted the traditional ceremony that is performed when a boy is sent to a school for the first time and all the members of the family were present. After the prayers invoking Saraswati — the goddess of learning — were chanted, the priest gave Naren a kind of red-tinged writing chalk called *Ram-khadi* to hold in his right hand. Then taking Naren's hand in his, he guided him to write on the ground the Bengali alphabets, pronouncing each as it was written.

Schools are places where one meets all sorts of children, and within a few days, Naren had acquired a vocabulary that quite upset his family's sense of propriety. So, his parents decided to take him out of the school, and, engaged a private tutor to conduct classes for him and his cousins and friends in the family worship-hall itself.

Naren's exceptional intelligence was soon noticed, and he learned to read and write when the other boys were still wrestling with the alphabets. His memory was prodigious. He had a peculiar way of learning. He would close his eyes and sit motionless or lie down when attending the classes. The private tutor who had been engaged did not understand this peculiarity of his charge, and one day he was provoked to shake Naren rudely to rouse him from his seeming sleepiness. Naren opened his eyes in wounded surprise to listen to the angry words of the tutor. Then, in self-defence, he recited word-to-word the whole text that had been read in the preceding hour. Thereafter, the tutor regarded him with admiration, for in his long experience with pupils, never had he come across one with such a remarkable memory.

Even at an early age Naren asserted himself as the leader of his group, and was 'king' among his playmates. Scurrying up the staircase from the ground floor, as he rushed towards the veranda of the *Puja* hall, he would proclaim 'I am the *Samrat*, the King of kings', and then, play-acting as the samrat, he would himself sit down on the landing and tell two of his fellows to stand on the steps before him as 'prime minister' and 'commander-in-chief'. He would then direct five others to stand a step or two lower as 'princes' of the kingdoms under his empire, and permitted his courtiers to sit one step lower than these 'princes'. He would then formally announce his '*durbar*', that is his court, as 'open'. Then one by one, the princes and the courtiers would prostrate themselves before their samrat and address him as 'Son of the Solar World, the Lord of Lands and Seas, and the Protector of *Dharma*, or religion.' The ceremony over, the samrat would then ask his princes and courtiers about the welfare of his empire and listen to the grievances of his subjects. A criminal would then be brought before him, and if the accusations against him were proved, 'His Majesty' would order his beheading, and then all the guards would spring upon the offender. As the samrat, Naren administered justice with royal dignity, and would frown upon the slightest insubordination, and this game of 'King and the Court' was his favourite.

The caste system — so very pronounced in those days — was a mystery to Naren. He was bewildered by the ban of the member of one caste to eat with a member of another or smoke his *hookah*, the Indian pipe, and wondered what would happen if one did. He decided to find out himself. One day he boldly entered the family smoking room, and took a whiff from each and every one of the hookahs kept for people of different castes. No, he was not dead! Just then his father entered, and asked him what he was doing in the smoking room, to which Naren replied, 'Oh, father! Why, I was trying to see what would happen if I broke caste! Nothing has happened!' Viswanath laughed heartily and with a knowing look on his face, walked into his private study. Naren's boyish exuberance thus expressed itself in all sorts of ways — naughty and otherwise.

There were some people who saw signs of Naren's future greatness even in his tender age. Kaliprasad, Naren's grand-uncle and once the head of the Dutta house, was on his deathbed in 1869.

When he found that he had only a few hours more to live, he called the whole family and asked the children if any one of them could read to him passages from the Mahabharata, so that his soul contained the thoughts of that great epic. Everyone was too shy to read aloud to the dying elder. But Naren, and one of his sisters, were not. Naren took up the heavy volume and read out the glories of the heroes and the Lord in a loud and clear voice. As he was reading the particular portion where Garuda flew off with his mother Vinata on his shoulders — symbolising the soul's rising on the wings of knowledge to blessedness — the breathing of Kaliprasad became slower and slower. Then he spoke in an undertone, but with the burning certainty of vision that the dying sometimes evince, 'Child, you have a great future ahead of you.' Having uttered these words, his soul passed away.

In 1871, Naren was admitted afresh to class 2 in the English section of Pandit Ishwar Chandra Vidyasagar's Metropolitan Institution, a famous school of those days. Naren was very restless in school and could not sit still for long, but both his teachers and classmates soon recognised his exceptional intelligence. He participated in all the games played in school, and was proficient in boxing and cricket. He disliked quarrelling and could not tolerate physical fights. He was kind at heart and would always be by the side of a sick classmate.

Naren's restlessness probably emanated from a tremendous dynamism, enormous energy, and immense aspiration that burst out in the form of high spirits, adventurousness, ardour, thirst for knowledge and travel, and dissatisfaction with monotony and stagnation. But even in the midst of extreme restlessness, he would occasionally be overwhelmed by some inspiration, as though his mind had travelled far away from his body. It was this dynamism that later took him around India, and then around the world. Much later, Swami Vivekananda had told one of his English disciples that during his childhood he used to become restless as he experienced an inexhaustible force rising inside his body, and this made him fidget about all the time, yearning to do something or the other.

Soon after his admission into the Metropolitan Institution, Naren was told that he would have to learn the English language. Initially, he was not willing to learn a foreign language before mastering his own mother tongue. It was after a lot of pestering by his teachers, his parents, and his confidant, the old relative Nrisimha Dutta, that he agreed to learn English. But once he agreed to learn the language, he studied it with all earnestness, and later mastered it to such an extent that his words and speeches in English have since become a new gospel.

Naren was still a devout admirer of wandering monks, and meeting them was always a pleasurable experience for him. He cherished a longing to become one himself someday, and in his boyish fervour he would show his friends his palm, and pointing out to certain lines therein — which an old man had once told him predicted his becoming a monk — he would tell them what he would do and where he would go once he became a mendicant.

Even at that tender age, Naren despised superstitions and never took anything at face value. This characteristic remained with him throughout his life, and it was this that prompted him even to question his Master, Sri Ramakrishna's claim to have seen God, or, even later, to declare, 'Do not believe a thing because you read it in a book. Do not believe a thing because another has said it so. Find out the truth for yourself. That is realisation.'

Naren was blessed with a prodigious memory and could memorise a book by reading it once. This made him the foremost student in his class and he still had time for play and fun. However, he studied strenuously two or three months before his examinations, in which he did well. He was particularly good in English, History and Sanskrit, but, like his father, had a distaste for Mathematics.

Naren had a flair for drawing and also possessed a melodious voice. He mingled with his classmates intimately and his personality attracted everyone towards him. He could outwit anyone in talking, had a wonderful presence of mind, and an endless capacity to extemporise. He would never be morose, knew how to make others laugh and kept all his classmates charmed. He was strong-minded and fearless. Truthfulness was the very backbone of his life, and his fun was always innocent. His liking for meditation grew with him.

Naren applied himself earnestly to physical culture, and gradually attained proficiency in *lathi* playing, or fencing with long sticks, rowing, swimming and wrestling. He had a special enthusiasm for *lathi* play. Ever averse to passivity, Narendranath always led an active life. If he were not busy at the gym, he would go out on his pony, which his father had bought for him. Riding was one of his favourite pastimes and gradually he mastered the art. He would even show magic-lantern pictures at home, and amused himself by making toy gaslights and aerated waters, which had been recently introduced in Calcutta. He even made toy railways and all sorts of machineries. He also learned to cook.

Naren loved his brothers and sisters dearly, and they reciprocated similarly. At night they would pester him for stories, and he would relate to them the ones he had heard from his mother and maternal grandmother. He was a fine storyteller and often acted out his characters.

Naren established some sort of a relationship with every family in his locality and all of them regarded him with fondness. He kept everybody amused with his ready wit and enthusiasm and was always there to console them at the time of any sorrow. Over a period of time, a change in his temperament was noticeable as he began to show a preference for intellectual pursuits. He started attending public lectures regularly, and surprised

his friends with his original criticism of whatever he heard or read. He turned out to be a good debater as well.

In 1877, when Naren was fourteen years old and studying in the then third class — equivalent to the present class eight — his father had to leave for Raipur in the Central Provinces. Since his professional work would keep him busy for a couple of years there, Viswanath called his family over.

In the absence of any direct transportation from Calcutta to Raipur in those days, the journey involved a fortnight's bullock cart travel through dense forests. Naren was thrilled with the adventure, and his heart was charmed with the boundless power and endless love of the Creator of such natural wonders. Once, he even lost consciousness of the external world for some time, and was transported to the world of deep meditation. Another characteristic of his was his feeling of familiarity with a new place or person, the impression of which/whom persisted, but which he was unable to recollect.

The absence of any school in Raipur, brought about greater intimacy between the son and the father, and Viswanath's noble mind attracted the intellect of his son. Viswanath believed that educating involved stimulating the mind and not superimposing ideas, and gave the boy intellectual freedom in his conversations with him even on serious topics demanding depth, precision and soundness of thought. Thus, Naren owed to his father his capacity for grasping the essentials of things, of delving into the depth of an issue, and holding the real issue under discussion. Many scholars would visit Viswanath, and Naren would listen to their discussions, and sometimes even join them. Viswanath was glad to see the elders often treat Naren on equal footing.

During the two years of stay at Raipur, Naren learned and mastered the game of chess, and was also taught the secrets and mysteries of the culinary art by his father. Viswanath also taught Naren songs of various kinds and on the family's return to Calcutta, arranged for Naren's training in classical vocal and instrumental music under reputed ustads. Naren mastered playing instruments like the *pakhawaj*, *tabla*, *esraj* and the *sitar*, but his forte was vocal music. He came to be known as an accomplished singer and was infatuated with singing. He practised for hours together in a small room on the first floor of his maternal grandmother's house on Simla Street and his companions would often assemble to listen to him. His own family was charmed with his voice, and he often sang to them, especially his father.

Naren would bring out the inherent spirit of a song, and singing became a wonderful means of worship for him. It was his singing that brought him to his Master, Sri Ramakrishna, who was so deeply moved by Naren's singing that he went into a *samadhi*, or trance.

Viswanath utilised the proximity that Raipur brought between him and his son to its hilt, and taught him some lessons in life too. On one occasion, Naren confronted his father with the question, 'What have you done for me?' and his father's reply was instant, 'Go, look at yourself in the mirror.' The son understood that his father was a king amongst men. Another time, Naren asked his father as to what were the elements of real good manners, to which his father replied, 'Never show surprise'. It was probably this man-to-man talk about life's intricacies that laid the foundations of Swami Vivekananda's walking with equal dignity amongst both the royals and the commoners later in life.

During his stay in Raipur, Naren had acquired a keen sense of personal dignity and when he returned to Calcutta in 1879 he showed changes in both his physique and temperament. He started being choosy about his friends and preferred those with an intellectual bent of mind. However, he remained large-hearted and generous.

On his return to Calcutta, there was some difficulty in getting readmission to his old school.

However, knowing his ability, the teachers made an exception in his case. Naren had to make up for the two years that he was absent from school, and also study for that year's entrance examination. He studied hard and was the only one in the Metropolitan Institution to clear the entrance in the first division that year. It was during this short second stint at the Metropolitan Institution, that he proved his oratory skills in the presence of none other than Sir Surendra Nath Banerjee, a foremost national leader of the time and an orator par excellence himself.

After passing his entrance examination at the age of sixteen, Naren joined the Arts faculty of the Presidency College in January 1880. Naren contracted malaria in the second year of college, as a result of which his attendance fell short and he was not allowed to appear for the First Arts (F.A.) examination. However, the General Assembly's Institution, founded by the Scottish General Missionary Board and now known as the Scottish Church College, sent him up for the F.A. examination.

A strict study routine before the examination helped Naren overcome the loss of time, and he cleared his F.A. examination in 1881 in the second division. He continued studying at the General Assembly's Institution till he cleared the Bachelor of Arts examination in 1884. After his return from the West in January 1897, the students of this very same Scottish Church College had un-harnessed the horses of Swami Vivekananda's carriage and drawn it themselves.

Narendranath studied English, History and Mathematics for his entrance course, and added Logic and Psychology for his F.A. examination. For his B.A. course, he substituted Logic and Psychology with Philosophy. He evinced a keen interest in Philosophy and Logic, and in some forms of higher Maths. He also made great efforts to master the English language, especially in the art of conversation and debating, both of which he excelled in.

Again, it was in General Assembly's Institution itself that Naren first heard about Sri Ramakrishna Paramahamsa from none other than the noted scholar Professor William Hastie, the then principal of the Institution. One day while explaining the

Principal W.W. Hastie.

meaning of trance as in Wordsworth's 'Excursion', Professor Hastie referred to Ramakrishna Paramahamsa of Dakshineswar. Later that year Naren met Sri Ramakrishna for the first time at Sri Surendra Nath Mitra's house at Simla Colony in Calcutta.

After the F.A. examination, Narendranath developed his own style of intellectual pursuit. His mind became intensely analytical and he subordinated imagination to the demands of reason. He was a born idealist and a seeker of truth, and beneath his conscious mind ran the strong desire for truth, or reality. He disliked foppishness and could not tolerate exhibitionism in manner or apparel. However, he remained as adventurous as ever and was the first to see the humorous side of a situation.

A story goes round about his improvisations in helping his compatriots. The General Assembly's Institution had the provision for waiver of fees for those who could substantiate their need. Haridas Chattopadhyaya, a classmate of Narendranath was in great financial difficulty and was not in a position to clear off his dues before the examination. Rajkumar, a senior clerk, had the power to take decisions in such matters, but he was not agreeing to waive Haridas's dues. Narendranath knew that Rajkumar was a regular visitor to an opium-smoking den, and one day, after college, Naren waited for Rajkumar there. When Rajkumar turned up at the den, Naren again made his plea on behalf of Haridas and added that if the request was ignored, he would publicise Rajkumar's visits to the opium den in the college. Rajkumar immediately conceded to the remission of the college dues and Haridas could thus sit for his exams.

Narendranath only gave such time to academic examinations as was absolutely necessary. The rest of his time and energy he spent on meditation, extracurricular studies, music, exercise, debates and discussions. He was not very keen on academic excellence, and was drawn to other pursuits.

Music was the second way of praying for Naren, and it gave him immense joy. He was not only a great singer, but also an authentic theoretician of music. He delved deeply in the science and art of vocal and instrumental music in a treatise in Bengali entitled *Sangit-Kalpataru*, which was published in 1857. He had written a masterly introduction to the book *Sangit-Sangraha*, a compilation of devotional and inspirational songs composed in various Indian languages. Later in life he even composed several songs and hymns that are, to this day, sung by the devotees at Ramakrishna Mission. Sometimes, he even danced along with his singing, and his dance movements were also very graceful.

Those were the days of the first stirrings of political awakening in India, and a nation's travail in passing through a new phase brought in its trail, movements of reform in various fields. The Brahmo Samaj, an outward expression of an endeavour to liberalise, and at the same time conserve the evolved traits of the Hindu race — as initiated by the eloquent Keshab Chandra Sen and inspired by Raja Ram Mohun Roy — drew Narendranath's attention. The progressive views of the Samaj, whose meetings Naren often attended, influenced his thought process, and he espoused the cause of the Samaj in all earnestness. However, the Brahmo Samaj split in 1878, and Naren joined the Sadharan Brahmo Samaj founded under the leadership of Pandit Shivnath Shastri and Vijay Krishna Goswami on 15 May that year. His intense desire for justification of the means to an end made him identify himself with anything that established equality and promised liberation from obsolete methods. Narendranath's versatile mind sought to encompass the entire range of the renaissance — religious, cultural and national — of his time.

Naren sat for his B.A. examinations in December 1883, and at the instance of his father, he joined the three-year law course at the then Metropolitan Institution, which is now known as Vidyasagar College. He even contemplated going to the Bar in England, which did not materialise due to the sudden death of his father.

It was all because of his father's foresight that as soon as Naren became twenty-one years of age, he got enrolled as a 'Freemason'. He attained the sublime degree of 'Master Mason' on 20th May 1884. It was a Freemason, G.C. Connor — whom Naren had met earlier at the Anchor and Hope Lodge in Calcutta — who introduced Swami Vivekananda to other Freemasons to tide over his difficult days in Chicago later in the year 1894.

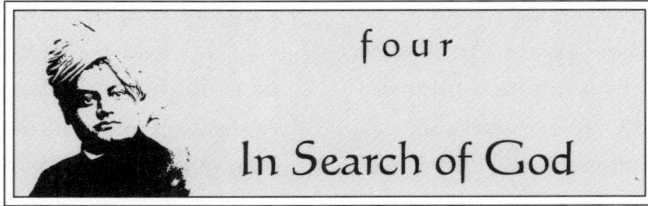

The principal ingredient of Naren's character was purity. Though still a boy, delighting in the ways of youthful life, he always avoided all devious routes. He always considered purity as the cardinal virtue, and the very basis of spiritual life. He realised the merit behind the great teaching of Jesus, 'Blessed are the pure in heart, for they shall see God'. He considered *brahmacharya*, or absolute abstinence, as ideal during one's student years.

In his youth, he was haunted by two opposite visions: while on the one hand he would visualise a wordly life of ease and luxury, on the other, he would see a *sanyasi* or a wandering monk, who had no earthly possessions, instead was conscious of the divine reality and was governed by God's will alone. He believed that he was capable of realising either of these two visions but his inner self gradually led him to the path of renunciation, while the worldly one began to fade until it finally disappeared.

The spiritual and intellectual atmosphere of the Brahmo Samaj satisfied him for some time, and he began to believe in the existence of a formless God with attributes, as against the 'Absolute' of the *Adwaita Vedanta*. However, he also believed that if God really existed, he would surely appear in answer to the sincere prayers of his devotees. It also began to dawn on him that if realisation of God was his goal, he was as far from it now as he was before joining the Samaj.

In his longing to know the Truth, Naren went to Maharshi Debendranath, Rabindranath Tagore's father and a leading member of the Brahmo Samaj — whom he had visited earlier also — and bluntly put forth the question 'Sir, have you seen God?' The venerable old man was startled both at the sudden appearance of Naren and also by his question, and could only say, 'My boy, you have the Yogi's eye.'

Naren came away disappointed. He went and posed the same question to the leaders of other religious sects, but to no avail. Not one of them could say that he had seen God. He then remembered Sri Ramakrishna for whom he had sung earlier at his neighbour Surendra Nath Mitra's house. On that occasion Ramakrishna had been greatly pleased with Naren's singing and had invited him to Dakshineswar. So Naren decided to go to Dakshineswar and put this question to him. As destiny would have it, one day in December 1881 Surendra Nath Mitra invited him to accompany him to Dakshineswar and Naren accepted the invitation.

Naren put the same question to Sri Ramakrishna that he had earlier put to Maharshi Debendranath. Sri Ramakrishna not only answered in the affirmative but went on to explain, 'Yes, I see Him just as I see you here, only in a much intense way. God can be realised, one can see and talk to Him as I am seeing and talking to you, but who cares? People shed torrents of tears for their wife and children, for wealth or property, but who does so for the sake of God? If one weeps sincerely for Him, He surely manifests Himself.'

Sri Ramakrishna's answer impressed Naren immensely. For the first time someone said that he had seen God, that religion was a reality to be felt and sensed. Though Naren considered Ramakrishna crazy, yet, sitting beside him, he felt a strange feeling of blessedness transmit through his entire mind and body.

The result of this meeting was the re-Hinduising of an agnostic soul by his master through his life and practice of the religion, which, as perceived by him, was for the moral and spiritual upliftment of all human beings, irrespective of caste, creed, nationality, or even religion. Naren understood that the greatest religion was to be true to oneself, to have faith in 'oneself', for 'if you do not exist, how can God exist? If I cannot think of God, He does not exist for me.' Naren was thus initiated by his master to perceive God as 'Existence-Knowledge-Bliss', *Sat-Chit-Anand*.

Sri Ramakrishna represented the old school of thought, with its spiritualism, asceticism and realisations emanating from the *Upanishads*, and Naren had the doubts and scepticism of the modern times, unwilling to accept even the highest religious truths without verification, yet seeking the Truth zealously. Naren was yet to learn that reason could not transport one's mind beyond relativity and into the 'absolute' where lay the Truth of Religion. But it was his contact with Sri Ramakrishna, and the subsequent happenings, that transformed him from Narendranath to Swami Vivekananda — the Hindu monk who walked upon the path of righteousness for the salvation of his soul, and for the good of the world, which in Sanskrit stands for *Atmano Mokshartham, Jagadhitaya Cha.*

Like Christ chose Peter to lay the foundation of the Church, Krishna transmitted the message of the *Gita* through Arjuna, and Buddha elected Ananda to spread the message of compassion — Sri Ramakrishna recognised Naren as the one who would carry his message to the world:

Leaving the different forms of life that exists before you, where art thee seeking God; he who loves all beings, is the one who serves God.

There were three factors that shaped Naren's character and destiny — his innate spiritual tendency, the influence of his family and studies, and the guidance of Sri Ramakrishna, his spiritual teacher.

Naren was aware of the intellectual pursuits of most philosophical systems, which kept out the

Surendranath Mitra (1850-1890).
(far left): Mahendra Nath Gupta (1854-1932) the author of the 'Gospel of Sri Ramakrishna'.

(opp.): Sri Ramakrishna in samadhi at a kirtan.

IN SEARCH OF GOD

study of human emotions and thereby blunted man's creative and responsive faculties. Thus, theological dogmas necessitating 'believing without understanding', and charting diagrams of Truth, did not interest him. He was in search of the real Truth. However, Herbert Spencer's philosophy of reasoning interested him, and he later on applied it to the teachings of the *Upanishads* and the *Vedanta*.

Naren was thus against the prevailing Hindu social system under the bondage of the priestly caste. He found the social segregations on the basis of caste and creed intolerable. His heart bled for the millions of poor and distressed, but he also visualised a bright future for the Indian race. He realised that Lord Krishna's messages harmonised Christianity's love, Islam's equality, and Buddhism's compassion. He advocated the discarding of the inherent defects in the different religious practices, and advised people to adopt the ways of the 'bee', seeking only the nectar, as against the 'fly' which sought ulcers. He emphasised that the prophets and other holy souls across time have been the milestones on the path of human progress and have always urged mankind to move forward; but it is the human race which, in spite of such teachings, has chosen to cling on to the time of the pronouncement of the respective doctrines, rather than the doctrine itself. To him, religion was a process and doctrines were like exercises to perfect the soul to accept God, and *dharma* had to be reorganised in consonance with modern needs and problems.

Naren accepted the fact that knowledge is gained through the interaction of objects and human senses, with time and space being the yardsticks. Thus, complete realisation of the inner self is impossible as it is not measurable in terms of either time or space. But Naren also understood that sense perceptions and deductions, which were mostly subjective in nature were also not reliable representations of the original experience. He realised that western thinkers failed to segregate the 'self' from 'objective consciousness', and therefore lagged behind in reaching the ultimate Truth. Nevertheless, he had great respect for western material science, and applied its analytical processes to test the various supernatural experiences of Sri Ramakrishna, and accepted only those that cleared the benchmark.

Sri Ramakrishna illuminated Naren's insatiable intellect. But Naren fought every inch of the way, and accepted something only when it was no longer rational to deny it. The sovereignty of Truth satisfied Naren's intellect and helped him overcome scepticism and materialism. Then came the hour of his darkest trial, to control the fascinations of the senses and the cravings of a youthful nature. He considered these as impure, gross and carnal and, after consciously overcoming them, developed a pure character with impassioned sensibilities. He practised meditation and would sometimes pass into his innermost recess, and Sri Ramakrishna's comforting words always steadied his mind's aberrations. Ramakrishna would ask him to be sincere in his pursuits, and to pray to God to reveal His real nature to him. He assured Naren that if he prayed sincerely, God will definitely listen to him.

These words of the Master encouraged Naren to delve more and more into the practice of spiritual exercises. He recollected Hamilton's demarcation of philosophy from religion, wherein intellect could gain only hints of the Truth of God but could not arrive at a correct knowledge of Him. Study, music and meditation kept his mind occupied.

Around this time, the financial position of the Duttas of Simulia, or Simla, deteriorated drastically, and the joint family also split. As a result, Viswanath had to leave the ancestral house with his family. He shifted to a rented house at 7, Bhairav Biswas Lane, a place very close to Naren's maternal grandmother's house.

Like all fathers, Viswanath wanted Naren to marry. However, Sri Ramakrishna was greatly opposed to the idea, and, strangely, every time there was any progress in the matter, some unforeseen difficulty would arise, and the matter had to be abandoned. But once Naren's father did succeed in finalising his marriage with the daughter of an influential and wealthy Bengali family of Calcutta who promised a handsome dowry as well. However, Naren refused to marry, and the wedding had to be cancelled due to the sudden demise of Viswanath himself.

Sri Ramakrishna envisaged Naren as the saviour of souls and could never accede to his being tied down to one person, or just one family. He was afraid that Naren would not be able to bear the importunities of his parents and relatives, and would give in to the bondage of a married life. Thus, if, for any reason, Naren failed to turn up at Dakshineswar for several consecutive days, the Master would himself go to him in Calcutta and counsel him for meditation and other spiritual exercises. Naren chose to remain a celibate and follow the life of a monk whose greatness, unlike that of the reputed, popular, wealthy or the powerful, was not destructible by death because the monk sought a reality that neither changed, nor was conditioned by it.

Naren's father, Viswanath Dutta died on 25th February 1884, and this brought Naren face to face with the grim reality of the world. Viswanath was the only earning member of the family, and his philanthropic ways had left the Duttas with no savings. Naren, being the eldest son, was now responsible for a family of seven, and he had no income. He was bewildered and often looked starvation in the face. In spite of this, he faced life with all determination and sacrificed as much as he could for the family. He gave up his articleship in the attorney's office and, for some time at least, worked as a teacher at the Metropolitan Institution, where he became the headmaster in June 1886.

During this time, Naren's relationship with his mother Bhuvaneswari Devi strengthened immensely. She showed exemplary adaptability to the sudden change of circumstances. Although used to spending a thousand rupees a month on household expenses when her husband was alive, she now took care of her sons, daughters and herself in just thirty rupees a month. But she was never dejected. Naren, however, could not bear to see the plight of his mother and siblings, and in his mind crept up doubts of the existence of God.

Memories of his experiences of the divine visions during his childhood which were now strengthened by his contact with Sri Ramakrishna, haunted him, and instilled the belief that God does exist, and that there must be a way to realise Him. Then, one night, he had a vision of some divine power unravelling the reality of the coexistence of divine justice and mercy, and the presence of misery in the creation of Blissful Providence. From that

Narendra meditating.

time onwards, Naren, like his grandfather, secretly started preparing to renounce the world. He even fixed a date for the purpose and was thrilled to learn that Sri Ramakrishna would be coming to Calcutta on that day itself. But as soon as Naren met Sri Ramakrishna, the latter asked him to accompany him back to Dakshineswar.

On reaching Dakshineswar, Sri Ramakrishna went into a trance and started singing a song that indicated that he was aware of Naren's intentions to renounce the world. Then later in the night, when they were alone, the Master called the disciple to his side and told him, 'I know you have come for the Mother's work, and wont be able to live a worldly life, but for my sake, stay in the world as long as I live.'

The next day Naren returned home, but his desperation to meet the needs of the family brought

him back to his guru. He knew that God listened to Sri Ramakrishna, and he also knew that the Master would not deny putting in a prayer to remove his monetary problems. The Master told Naren that he had done it so many times, but since Naren did not 'accept' the Mother Kali of the temple, she has not granted his prayer. He edged Naren to go inside the temple himself on that Tuesday night and ask of Her any boon and he was sure that the Mother would grant him the same. Naren believed his Master and went inside the temple, and found the image of the Divine Mother. A feeling of bliss descended on him, and Naren forgot about the world, and prayed for the boons of discrimination, renunciation, knowledge and devotion, and an 'uninterrupted vision of Thee'. When Naren came out of the temple, the Master enquired if he had prayed for the removal of his earthly problems, and he could reply only in the negative. The Master urged him to go again, which he did but this time he prayed for love and devotion. The Master chastised him and sent him a third time, whence a remorse came over Naren. He felt that asking the Mother for pecuniary means was like asking a gracious king for mere vegetables. This time he prayed for knowledge and devotion. He realised that this was due to his Master's charm over him and he insisted that the Master grant him a boon so that his people at home do not suffer the pangs of poverty any more. After much persuasion, the Master gave in and blessed him saying that they will never be in want of plain food and clothing.

This incident was a landmark in the life of Naren who had always had only contempt for image worship. But this incident helped him find the meaning and purpose of worshiping God through images and he also realised the concept of Mother as God. Sri Ramakrishna was delighted to see this transformation in him.

The idol of Goddess Bhavatarini at Dakshineswar.

The company of Sri Ramakrishna was a lesson in austerity and spiritual discipline. It was not easy to understand the earthly philosophy of the Master, and one needed immense concentration to enter the sphere of divine emotion. Unlike elsewhere, the master-disciple relationship here was a tender, easy, natural and human one, and the atmosphere was divine. Yet, it was through fun and play that the Master moulded the spiritual life of his disciples.

The Master could clearly discern the latent spiritual power of his disciples, and would encourage them to channelise these in the right direction. He would warn them if they went astray, and controlled them by silently and unobtrusively observing every minute detail of their lives. The solitude of the *panchvati* at the Dakshineshwar temple — which itself was situated on the banks of the Ganga — helped the disciples in meditating, and the Master helped them in their spiritual exercises. The Master also joined them in their fun and merry-making for example, in picnics.

At Dakshineshwar, Naren felt as if he was reliving his childhood days, and he was at his boisterous best. All his pent up energy, which had tortured him earlier due to its not being released fully, now had a free hand and thus manifested itself as a torrent of spiritual energy. Sri Ramakrishna understood the flights of Naren's soul, and let his mind evolve itself to become its own master. He allowed Naren to doubt him and to try him, and advised him, 'It is not in assent or dissent that the goal is to be attained, but in actual and concrete realisation.'

It can safely be said that Naren alone understood the greatness of Sri Ramakrishna, whom he dared to doubt while all the others accepted every word uttered by him. Naren was the only disciple who despite having the highest reverence and adoration for him, accepted his teachings only after he was satisfied with the element of truth in it. Sri Ramakrishna also realised the inherent potentiality of Naren and would tell the other devotees about Naren's fathomless insight that the Mother herself could not gauge due to the boon that She had granted Naren. He would also tell them that Naren was in possession of eighteen extraordinary powers, just one or two of which were enough to make a man famous in the whole world.

Sri Ramakrishna's method of teaching was unique. He would teach through his body language, and through parables and songs, whose basis was that 'when realisation comes into the heart, all arguments cease and divine knowledge shines forth.' Having actually seen the Truth of this universe, Sri Ramakrishna had little use for logic. The man who preached universal love and tolerance actually lived it too. Sincerity was the main theme of his teaching, and he would say, 'Pray in any way, for the Lord hears even the footfall of an ant.' Worshipping anything in which the devotee saw his God manifesting was perfectly acceptable

to him. Sri Ramakrishna believed that human beings were the manifestation of God Himself and advocated 'service to man' as sheer worship of the Lord. The Hinduism that Sri Ramakrishna practiced was a positive, practical and living realisation.

The Master's teachings awakened Naren's realisation and he took it upon himself to embrace this essence of true Hinduism, and not the sectarian

The Panchavati at Dakshineswar where Sri Ramakrishna and later, his disciples practised many spiritual disciplines.
(right): Sri Ramakrisha's room at Cossipore.

(opp.): Sri Ramakrisha.

Hinduism as preached by most, to the world at large. The Master transformed the questioning Naren into his most trusting and understanding disciple. Naren was apprised of the 'existence, knowledge and Absolute Bliss' of Sachchidananda, and assured that there could never be any excess in one's love for God, and therefore, there was no harm in intense meditation. So Naren, who till then sang only those songs that praised the formless *Brahma*, now started singing those that brought about the intense spiritual love of Radha.

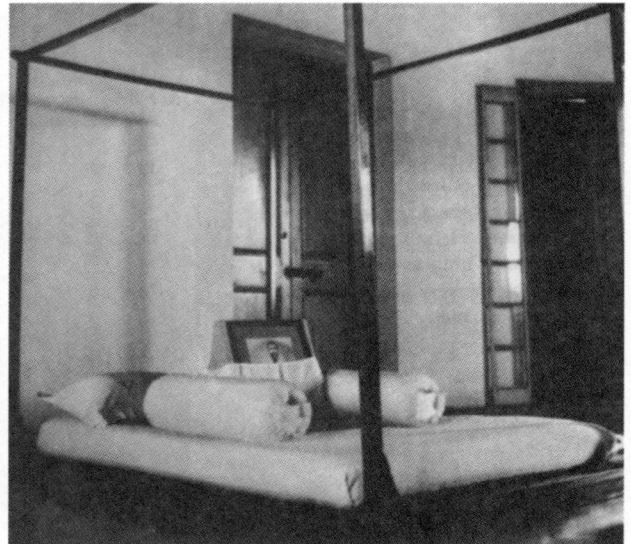

The Master's belief in the great future of Naren had an invigorating effect on him. He became conscious of the infallibility of the predictions of a Master whose spiritual greatness surpassed all forms of tests by physicians and philosophers alike. The Master ensured the all-round development of Naren, who, while physically appearing to be a young man full of vigour and vitality, was graceful and resolute in nature. He had the temperament of a genius and had an intense aloofness about himself. He was a philosopher by nature, and Sri Ramakrishna's love transformed him into a devotee as well. Naren's spirituality evolved from intellectual insight, as tempered and softened by divine love. He was virtually enslaved by the great selfless love that the Master had for him, which went to the extent of the Master once telling him 'O my Naren, do you know that I would do anything for you, even go about begging from door to door?'

Naren's character was moulded by both the sorrows and the great associations that he had had. Whereas poverty had taught Naren to sympathise with the poor, he learnt the difference between intellect and spirituality from his Master. Sri Ramakrishna perfected these two sides of Naren's character and moulded him into the vision he had of him, which manifested later on as Swami Vivekananda. Sri Ramakrishna knew that Naren's was the path of renunciation and guided him towards that end. He would warn him of the effects that lingered on with those who have renounced life after leading a worldly life, and forbade him to associate himself with such people. He told Naren that devotion to God could only be had through the purity of heart. In Swami Vivekananda's own words, whereas the 'Master was all *bhakti* without, but within he was all *gyan*, I am all *gyan* without, but in my heart all is *bhakti*.'

Naren's education from his Master continued throughout the five years he was in contact with him. Each visit to Dakshineshwar intensified the relationship further, and helped him absorb the Master's ideas and ideals. Naren was the son destined to inherit the treasure of *gyan* and *bhakti* from his Master. He envisaged his Master's life as the demonstration of the means to all spiritual ends, to the realisation of the Truth of the Universe itself. He saw in him a new Chaitanya, a new Shankaracharya, a new Buddha, whose teachings would rejuvenate Hinduism.

In the fifth and last year of their association, the Master developed some prolonged and incurable disease of the throat. There was a lot of speculation as to what caused it, but all the devotees were convinced that their goal of life was to follow his example and to serve him, and they took this as an opportunity to serve their beloved Master in whichever way they could. Naren began to visualise the inseparability of the human Sri Ramakrishna and the divine one, but he was pained at the deteriorating condition of his Master's health. By December, the Master was practically immobilised, and Naren and his eleven other fellow devotees stood guard over him round the clock.

Due to the administering of some new medicines by another doctor, the Master started feeling a little better in January 1886 and one day, he expressed a desire to stroll in the garden. There, he reached the highest pinnacle of spirituality and blessed all and sundry for the fulfilment of their wishes. Sri Ramakrishna quietly prepared Naren as the leader of the group of twelve disciples, who were to devote their lives to the carrying out of his mission, but Naren's mind was preoccupied with the Master's illness. He knew that whatever he had to learn or achieve, he had to do it fast. He developed his skills in meditation, and soon started realising his inner powers, but the

Master warned him of starting to 'spend before accumulating.'

Sri Ramakrishna's health again started sinking, but in spite of it all he appeared cheerful, thanks to the realisation that it was only a suffering of the body and could not take away his mental bliss. It was only towards the end of his life, in March 1886 that Naren finally realised that his Guru was part of the Mother herself. Naren led the other

day he called all the disciples, but Naren, and instructed them to follow Naren, and called Naren separately and entrusted the eleven others to him. Again, on another day, the Master called Naren and, looking steadfastly at him, went into meditation. Naren felt as if an electric shock passed through him for sometime, and then he found the Master weeping and saying that he has given everything to Naren and has become a *fakir* himself. He told

devotees through the days of devotion, sorrow, service, and ecstasy and they in turn were also untiring in their attention towards the Master.

The Master's health worsened towards the end of July 1886, and this evoked the maximum number of visitors, who came seeking his blessings, throughout August. The disciples were grief stricken at this condition of the Master, who was both their father and guide, who loved them all as a mother loves her children. The Master also resolved to pass on everything he possessed to the disciples, particularly Naren, whom he would summon every evening to his room and impart the final instructions on spiritual practices, of keeping his brother-disciples together, and how to guide and train them in their life of renunciation. Then one

Naren, 'By the force of power transmitted by me, great things will be done by you, only after that will you go where you came from.' A few days later, in the early hours of 16th August 1886, the Master entered into his *mahasamadhi* and left his mortal body. A spirit of calm resignation descended on the disciples, who were still to accept the departure of their Master.

Disciples at Cossipore after Sri Ramakrishna's demise. (right): Sri Ramakrishna's memorial.

six

The Beginnings of the Ramakrishna *Math* and Mission

Sri Ramakrishna left behind two kinds of devotees — the twelve disciples who had renounced the world in search of Truth, and the householders who paid for the expenses. As could be expected, the *mahasamadhi* of the Master brought about strife between the two groups regarding the place of internment of the holy ashes. Whereas Ram *babu* led the householders' demand of laying the holy ashes inside his Kankurgachi retreat — which would be dedicated to the memory of the Master and open to all for worship — Naren and his brother-disciples wanted to fulfil the Master's wishes and build a place for the relics on the banks of the Ganges. A controversy arose, but then Naren reasoned that they themselves did not have an address of their own, so the disciples agreed to part with a portion of the ashes to be kept at Ram *babu's* retreat, keeping the rest with themselves which would be preserved later at a place they would build one day. Accordingly, on *Janmastami* day, which fell on 23rd August that year, the urn carrying the ashes was taken in a procession to the Kankurgachi *Yogodyan* where it was laid to rest with due ceremony.

The householders did not approve of the idea of the twelve disciples resolving to lead the life of renunciation. They also opined that Sri Ramakrishna did not preach the monastic ideal and therefore there was no need to establish a monastery. There was difference of understanding among the young disciples also, and not all of them felt the need to spread the Master's message in the world, or to serve humanity. Some of them were in favour of realising God first. But Narendranath held that the monks should serve mankind in a spirit of worship, which itself would lead to the realisation of God.

However, this path brought forth sufferings unto them, which moved the Holy Mother Sarada Devi to pray to Sri Ramakrishna to fulfil the monks' basic requirements of food and shelter so that they could concentrate on preaching his teachings. It is said that soon after this, Sri Ramakrishna appeared one day before Surendra Nath Mitra, one of his householder devotees, and instructed him to make immediate arrangements for the young disciples. Surendra Nath immediately went to Naren's home, and narrating what happened, offered to rent a house for them, which they could then convert into a shrine for the Master. Naren was elated at the turn of events, and started searching for a house.

Vivekananda in Belgaum, October 1892.

Naren finally found one at Baranagar, a place between Dakshineswar and Calcutta. It was an old house and in such a bad condition that it needed extensive repairs. But on the other hand, it was expansive and had an outhouse that could be easily converted into a shrine for the Master. It also had the reputation of being haunted, so was available at a very cheap rent. In addition, it was ideally situated near the Ganga and the Cossipore burning *ghat* where the body of the Master was cremated. The peace and solitude of the area provided a perfect environment for their meditation.

Thus the monastery came into existence within six weeks of the Master's soul leaving his body. Naren became the true mouthpiece of the Master and his brother-disciples' love for him soon grew into reverence. They did not forget the Master's advice to them, and readily accepted Naren as their leader. However, it was at Matangini Devi's house at Antpur — a remote village near Haripal, enroute Tarakeswar — where they went during the Christmas vacation of 1886, that the monastic spirit flared up within them, and each of the nine disciples present there visualised a world of spiritual force in the other while subtly knitting them together.

The Ramakrishna brotherhood gathered momentum at Antpur and found its logical beginning one winter evening under the clear night sky and in front of a sacred fire. After meditation, Naren started telling the story of Jesus, beginning with the mystery of his birth to a maiden, his death, and his resurrection. The brother disciples could see in Naren the fervour of Paul's determination

Baranagore Math.

to spread the words of Christ even in the face of adversities. Naren exhorted them to become a Christ, to realise God and help in the redemption of the world, and to renounce it as Christ had done. The monks later on discovered that all discussion had happened on Christmas Eve. Even today, Christmas is celebrated with a lot of fervour at the Ramakrishna Mission headquarters at Belur *Math*.

Things started shaping up soon after their return to Calcutta from Antpur. While Naren was there at the *Math* since its very inception — Shashi, Sarat, Sarada, Niranjan and Baburam — one after the other, all these disciples left their homes for good and came to live at the Baranagar *Math*. Rakhal returned from Monghyr and joined them in January 1887, while Gangadhar joined as late as June 1890 after his pilgrimage to Tibet. Latu, alias Rakhturam, came from Vrindavan to join the *Math*, and so did Yogen who came back with the Holy Mother after the *tirth yatra*, or pilgrimage. Hari joined sometime in 1887, and Hariprasanna came much later in 1896, by which time the *Math* had shifted to Alambazar, even nearer to Dakshineshwar. Narendranath was at the helm and guided his brother disciples in the

affairs of the Mission for three more years, after which he became a wandering monk.

The *Math* was at the Baranagar premises from 1886 to 1892, whereupon it shifted to Alambazar. In 1897 it moved into the garden-house of Nilambar Mukherjee at Belur, which is now known as the Old *Math*. In December 1898, it moved to its present site at Belur itself, albeit a little northward. The spacious site at Belur on the west bank of Ganga was chosen by Swami Vivekananda himself, and it was he who carried and installed the Master's relics there on 9th December 1898, and the monastery was housed therein from January 1899. The mission of the Ramakrishna Order was twofold, to spread the teachings of *Vedanta* as embodied in the life of Sri Ramakrishna, and to improve the social conditions of the Indian people.

It was Swami Vivekananda's desire to erect a big memorial temple dedicated to the Master at Belur *Math*. Swami Vigyananand, who was an engineer before joining the order, was entrusted with the planning of the memorial, and he, in turn, consulted a noted European architect of Calcutta. They prepared a design of the proposed temple, which was

approved by Swami Vivekananda. But Swami Vivekananda's premature death in 1902 found the project in the cold storage. However, some thirty years after the demise of Swamiji, some of his devoted American students came forward with help to construct the grandiose memoriam of Sri Ramakrishna at Belur, whose foundation stone was laid in 1935 by none other than Swami Vigyananand who was then the vice-president of the order. The temple was completed in 1938, and it was again Swami Vigyananand, who as the President of the Ramakrishna Order performed the dedication of the temple and the consecration of the marble image of Sri Ramakrishna therein amidst imposing rites on 14th January that year. This was witnessed by about 50,000 devotees and spectators.

Group at Baranagore Math in 1887; Standing (left to right): Swamis Shivananda, Ramakrishnananda, Vivekananda, Premananda, Deben Majumdar, Mahendra Nath Gupta, Swami Trigunatitananda, and Mustaphi; Sitting (left to right): Swamis Niranjanananda, Saradananda, Brahmananda, and Abhedananda. (right): The Cossipore Garden.

(opp.): Belur Math on the west bank of Ganga. (inset): Sri Ramakrishna temple, Belur Math.

The unique architecture of the magnificent temple incorporates the basic architectural features of the religious places of all the established religions. Today, the Ramakrishna Mission has about ninety centres across the country through which it carries on various philanthropic activities, including educational work, medical services and relief work. The foreign centres, spread across the United States, United Kingdom, France, Switzerland, Argentina, Mauritius, Fiji, Singapore, Sri Lanka and Bangladesh, are devoted mainly to the spread of Sri Ramakrishna's teachings

It was sometime in January 1887 that Naren sought the opinion of his brother-disciples on going through the rituals of initiation as a *sanyasi* as prescribed by the scriptures. They gladly agreed to his proposal, and it was on a day in the third week of January that Kali — who had already obtained the mantras for performing the *Viraja-yagna* and other matters connected with the *sanyas* rites from a *sanyasi* of the Puri denomination — chanted the mantras as Naren and the other disciples repeated them and offered the oblations. This ceremony ritually confirmed the one conducted earlier by Sri Ramakrishna when he gave them ochre clothes at Cossipore and made them monks. Rakhal became Swami Brahmanand; Baburam, Swami Premanand; Shashi, Swami Ramakrishnaanand; Sarat, Swami Saradanand; Niranjan, Swami Niranjanand; Kali,

Swami Abhedanand; and Sarada, Swami Trigunatitanand. Tarak became Swami Shivanand, and Gopal senior, Swami Adwaitanand. Later on, Latu became Swami Adbhutanand and Yogen, Swami Yoganand. Hari (Chatterjee) ordained in 1887 and became Swami Turiyanand, while Gangadhar became Swami Akhandanand in 1890. Subodh joined the *sanyasis* as Swami Shubodhanand. Hariprasanna, when he renounced the world and joined the Mission in 1896, adopted the name Swami Vigyananand. These fifteen *sanyasis* are considered to be the direct disciples of Sri Ramakrishna. Of these Sri Ramakrishna had identified Narendra, Rakhal, Baburam, Yogen, Niranjan and one more, probably Hari Prasanna, as *Iswar-Kotis*, or members of the inner most circle of the Incarnation, that is, they have to take birth whenever the Incarnation is born.

Naren was inclined to take the name Swami Ramakrishnanand himself, but seeing Shashi's devotion to Sri Ramakrishna, he let him have that name. According to Swami Abhedanand, Naren had initially taken the name of Swami Vividishanand, which he seldom used. It was during his days as a wandering monk, and in order to prevent his brother disciples from following him, that he changed his name first to Swami Vivekananda in February 1891, and then to Swami Sachchidanand in October 1892. But, it was perhaps at the request of the Maharaja of Khetri, that on the eve of his departure for the West in May 1893, he once again adopted the name of Swami Vivekananda.

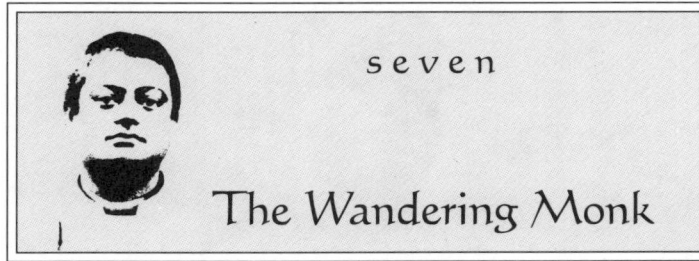

seven

The Wandering Monk

With the Order of the Ramakrishna being consolidated, Narendranath was torn between loyalty to the *Math* and its mission, and his yearning to be a wandering monk. After the demise of Sri Ramakrishna, and till July 1890, Narendranath spent most of the time with his monastic brothers.

Narendranath believed that a *sanyasi* could not be tied to a particular place, and he began to feel that the monastery was like a shackle which was impeding his progress in the realisation of God. Therefore he resolved to break away from it and wander into the unknown realms of humanity. Earlier, his absences from the *Math* were for short durations, and something or the other brought him back. However, when he left the monastery in July 1890, he came back only in February 1897 after his triumphant return visit to the West.

The very appearance of Narendranath in the saffron robe with a *kamandalu* or an ascetic's water pot, in one hand and the *danda* or staff in the other, made him conspicuous wherever he went. He travelled mainly on foot, or by a vehicle whose driver was hospitable, or by train if someone bought the ticket for him. Although he did not keep any notes of his journeys, the turn of events indicate that Varanasi was the first city he visited.

At Varanasi, the home of monks, the centre of learning and the seat of Lord Shiva, Swamiji met many scholars and *sanyasis* and exchanged ideas with them. The sacred Ganges, the praying votaries, the atmosphere of holiness, the temples of Viswanath and Annapurna, the knowledge that both Buddha and Shankaracharya had preached there, made vivid impressions on him. He also visited nearby Sarnath, where Buddha had preached the first of his sermons. Swamiji had a unique experience during his stay at Varanasi. It taught him a lesson, which years later, he recounted in a lecture in New York. It was a simple experience with monkeys, who shrieked and howled and chased him. He sought refuge in a temple, but, when on acting upon the advice of an old *sanyasi* who was passing by, he accosted them, they fled. Swamiji referred to this incident as a lesson for life, and advised people to 'face any situation boldly, and then, like the monkeys, the hardships of life fall back ...'

Next, he visited Ayodha, which was the birthplace of Lord Rama and also the kingdom where Ram had introduced *Ram-rajya*. From

Vivekananda during his days as a wandering monk.

Ayodha he went to Lucknow, where he was awestruck by the splendours erected by the Oudh dynasty. His next stop was Agra, where the Taj Mahal filled him with wonder. After Agra it was Vrindavan, the erstwhile abode of Lord Krishna, and there Swamiji was in ecstasy.

Swamiji planned to go to Haridwar from Vrindavan, and, in that direction, he approached the Hathras railway station where he found his first disciple in Sarat Chandra Gupta, the assistant station master there. Sarat Chandra was so enamoured by Swamiji's personality and preaching, that he gave up his job, renounced the world, and

where he stayed for almost a year before he set out for another sojourn, this time first to Baidyanath Dham in Bihar.

However, the news of the illness of another brother-disciple at Allahabad made Swamiji change his itinerary from Varanasi to Allahabad, the city of the confluence of the Ganga, Yamuna and the mythological Saraswati. From Allahabad, Swamiji went to Ghazipur to meet Pawhari Baba, a master in the *Adwaita Vedanta* system. It was probably at Ghazipur that Swamiji had the first opportunity to give his treatise on the *Sanatana Dharma* to some European officials who had come to meet him, and

joined Swamiji in his wanderings. Thus, accompanied by Sarat, Swamiji moved on to Hrishikesh.

At Hrishikesh, the Swami and his disciple lived in the company of other *sadhus*, and passed their time in spiritual disciplines. The murmuring of the Ganges and the beckoning of the Himalayas elated Swamiji. However, fate had other plans — Sarat fell ill seriously and both of them returned to Hathras, where Swamiji also fell ill. At the insistence of his brother-disciples, Swamiji had to return to Calcutta,

who, after listening to him, encouraged him to go to Europe to preach his ideas. At Ghazipur he also had an experience that strengthened his mind against longing for great men any more, and to devote himself to single-minded meditation. From Ghazipur, Swamiji went back to Varanasi, where death of Balaram Bose — a great lay devotee of the

Varanasi: View of a ghat.
(right): Balaram Bose (1842-1890).

Master — on 13th April 1890, sent him back to Calcutta.

With the death of Surendra Nath Mitra — another great lay devotee of the Master and a benefactor of the *Math* — on 25th May, the brotherhood experienced a financial crunch. Girish Ghosh, Mahendra Nath and some others did extend help heartily, but it was not sufficient. So the monks decided to lead a wandering life and thus reduce the expenses of the *Math*.

This time Swamiji stayed in the monastery for about three months, and then he set out again in the third week of July, with the same old determination of not returning until the time he had achieved his spiritual goal. This time, at least

in the initial phase, Gangadhar or Swami Akhandanand, whom Swamiji affectionately addressed as 'Ganges', accompanied him. Their first halt was Bhagalpur, where they put up at Manmatha Nath Chowdhury's place. Manmatha *Babu* was a staunch Brahmo who was 're-Hinduised' by Swamiji's eloquence and spirituality. Swamiji also interacted with the Jain monks at the temple of Nathanagar, and found out the relationship between Jainism and Buddhism. Their next stop was Baidyanath Dham, which Akhandanand had not visited earlier. From there they went to

Ghazipur, and, after that, to Varanasi and then to Ayodha, where they met Mahant Janakibar Saran, a scholar of Sanskrit and Persian.

The next place on Swamiji's itinerary was Nainital and from there they reached Almora enroute Badrikashram. One day, Swamiji was meditating under a *peepul* tree at a place called Kakrighat, situated about fourteen miles away from Almora at the confluence of the two rivers Koshi and Swial, when he experienced seeing 'the whole universe within an atom'. It was also near Almora that Swamiji came across a solitary cave where he started performing the most severe forms of spiritual practice in search of Truth. However, he felt the impetus to work, and this forced him into the realisation of the mission that he was to fulfil. At Almora Swamiji met Saradananda and another devotee of the Master, and the four left Almora together for Garhwal on their way to Badrinath dham. However, the government had

(left): View of Almora.

Swami Sadananda: Vivekananada's first disciple.

closed the road to Badrinath, and Swamiji and his entourage, after wandering in the Garhwals and Tehri, finally reached Dehradun about two months later.

Swamiji once again went to Hrishikesh from Dehradun. He had an attack of diphtheria, and was saved by a *sadhu*. The *Dewan* of Tehri was passing by Hrishikesh at that time, and on learning about Swamiji's illness visited him and referred him to a *hakim* or a Mohammedan doctor in Delhi. But Swamiji proceeded to Hardwar first, then to Saharanpur, and then to Meerut where his reunion with Swamis Akhandanand, Brahmanand, Saradanand, Turyianand, Adwaitanand and Kripanand at the Sheth-ji's garden — that is, where they were living — transformed it into a second Baranagar *Math*. They passed their time in meditation, prayer, in singing devotional songs, and by studying the scriptures and other literature in Sanskrit and English.

After some weeks, Swamiji again grew restless for self-realisation and solitude. He told his brother disciples that he had received the command of God regarding his future, and bade them adieu on his way to become a solitary monk. He left his devoted brethren at Meerut and proceeded all alone to Delhi. This was sometime in the latter half of January 1891.

The crisp winter air, the imperial bearings of the city, and its long history as the capital of India, both under Hindu and Muslim dynasties, impressed the learned monk greatly. In order to give his brother-disciples a slip, Swamiji had adopted the name Vividishananda at that time. But, in spite of this, his brother-disciples, now visiting Delhi, heard of an English speaking Hindu monk and were glad to see him. But Swamiji was not happy at their seeking him out, and he bluntly told them so.

Swamiji then set out for Rajasthan. His first stop there was the erstwhile princely kingdom of Alwar. At the state dispensary he met the doctor-in-charge, who happened to be a Bengali. He guided Swamiji to a room in the local market where the Swami could put up, and introduced him to a Muslim friend of his who was a teacher of Urdu and Persian at the local high school. Soon, the news of Swamiji's depth in religious matters spread by word of mouth and the increasing daily gathering forced his hosts to shift him to the house of Pandit Shambhunath, a retired engineer of the Alwar state. Both Hindus and Muslims of various castes and sects, and belonging to different social strata came to him, and Swamiji treated them all alike. Many of them became his devotees and he would partake many of his meals at the houses of his Muslim followers too.

Not long thereafter, the *Dewan* of the Maharaja of Alwar heard about Swamiji, and he invited the Swami to his house. After meeting him, the *Dewan* was convinced that Swamiji was the only person who could do some good to his Maharaja, who had become much anglicised in thought and manners. Accordingly, a meeting was arranged between Swamiji and Maharaja Mangal Singh*ji* of Alwar. Swamiji's boldness was a perfect match for the Maharaja's brashness, and soon the Maharaja was enamoured by the Swami's intelligence.

Swamiji cleared the Maharaja's aversion to idol worship in a unique way. He first asked the *Dewan* to get the photograph of the Maharaja, which was hanging on the wall, and then asked him to spit on it. Neither the *Dewan* nor any of the other servants of the Maharaja would do so, and the *Dewan* actually protested against the Swami's order. Swamiji then said that like the Maharaja's photograph, which was not the Maharaja himself but definitely reminded the *Dewan* and the others of the Maharaja's presence, the idol reminded the devotee of his God incarnate and he worshipped Him in the idol and not the idol as such. The Maharaja was overcome at this explanation and asked Swamiji to forgive him, to which Swamiji advised him to pray to God for His mercy.

Next on Swamiji's itinerary was the kingdom of Jaipur, where he stayed for two weeks. Here, Swamiji became very intimate with Sardar Hari Singh, the Commander-in-Chief of the state, at whose place he spent some days discussing spiritual and scriptural matters. From Jaipur, Swamiji moved on to Ajmer, a city replete with memories of the magnificence of its Hindu and Muslim rulers, and the seat of the *dargah* of the Muslim saint Moinuddin Chisti, who is revered by both Muslims and Hindus alike. From Ajmer, Swamiji proceeded to Mount Abu, site of the famous Jain temples or the Dilwara Temples, an architect's delight.

It was here in Mount Abu that Swamiji came across the Raja of Khetri, who went on to become

but it was the society that enforced such divisions to suit itself. Jagmohan was dumbfounded at both Swamiji's reply and the radiance emanating from him, and he invited Swamiji to meet his king.

According to the state diary of the Khetri state, the first meeting of Raja Ajit Singh of Khetri with Swamiji took place in the presence of Hardayal Singh of Jodhpur on 4th June 1891. Over the next few days, the Raja broached various subjects to Swamiji. Swamiji also sang on several occasions, and met many royal guests. His words of wisdom influenced the Raja beyond imagination and he begged Swamiji to come to Khetri with him and give him an opportunity 'to serve … with my whole heart'.

one of his greatest devotees. It was the Muslim pleader of the Maharaja of Kota who first met Swamiji in a cave in the rocks of the mountain. He was greatly influenced by Swamiji's learning, and pleaded with him to come and stay at his bungalow. At this bungalow came Munshi Jagmohanlal, the private secretary to the Raja of Khetri. At Jagmohanlal's query as to how a Hindu monk could stay at a Muslim's place, Swamiji replied that neither God nor the scriptures envisaged such divisions,

Accordingly, Swamiji left Mount Abu with the Raja of Khetri, and after travelling through Jaipur, Khairthal and Kota, they reached Khetri on 7th August 1891. Satisfied with the spiritual inclination of the Raja, Swamiji gave the Raja several lessons in

Maharaja Ajit Singh of Khetri.
The palace of the Maharaja of Khetri where Vivekananda stayed. It now houses the Ramakrishna Mission centre.

(opp.): Nakki Lake, Mt. Abu.

spirituality. Swamiji was much moved by the depth and sincerity of the Raja, and he became one of the few privileged ones to receive Swamiji's letters even from America.

At Khetri a chance encounter with a nautch girl taught Swamiji a very valuable lesson. One night, the Raja had brought over a nautch girl to entertain his guests, Swamiji being one of them. But Swamiji declined to go and watch her perform. This saddened the girl and she started singing a composition of the *Vaishnav* saint Surdas, a couplet which stressed on the manifestation of the One in all beings. Swamiji realised that he could therefore not discriminate against any one. He immediately went to the hall where the guests had gathered.

Swamiji was at Khetri for more than two-and-a-half months, and left for Ajmer on 27th October 1891. After spending about two weeks here, Swamiji probably left for the then Bombay Presidency, now bifurcated into the provinces of Gujrat and Maharashtra. The first known destination of Swamiji here was Ahmedabad, earlier known as Karnavati and one of the handsomest cities of India. Swamiji was awed by the Jain temples, and had some positive interactions with the local Jain scholars.

He was also fascinated by the splendour of the architecture and culture of the Sultans of Gujrat, under whose reign, Ahmedabad had served as the capital.

Swamiji's next stop was Limbdi where he went via Kathiawar. The Ranik Devi *sati* temple at Kathiawar made him aware of the traditional Hindu emphasis on the sanctity of marriage. At Limbdi he was also virtually waylaid by a degenerate sect of sex-worshippers in the garb of *sadhus* and had to be rescued by Thakore Sahib Jaswant Singh, the prince of the state. Later on Thakore Sahib was greatly impressed by Swamiji's preaching on *Vedanta*, and gave him the idea of going to the West, he himself having visited England and America a few years earlier.

After leaving Limbdi, Swamiji went to Junagadh via Bhavnagar and Sirohi. He had now become more cautious, be it with respect to choosing a place to stay, or mixing with people. Thakore Sahib had given him a letter of introduction, and at Junagadh he was the guest of Haridas Viharidas Desai, the *Dewan* of the state. The Ashoka Stone, — situated on the outskirts of the town — had the inscriptions of Emperor Ashoka and was of great interest to Swamiji. He also visited the nearby pilgrimage Girnar, a conglomeration of about ten hills, the highest of which is known as Gorakhnath. Girnar is sacred to the Buddhists, the Jains and the Hindus alike, and ten thousand odd steps, cut in the rocks, lead to the many Jain and Hindu temples built on the different hills. It was at Junagadh itself that Swamiji met his brother disciple Abhedanand. Abhedanand was also wandering around in Gujarat at that time, and when he heard that a monk matching Swamiji's description was around, he sought him out and met him. From Junagadh, Swamiji made a short trip to Bhuj in the Kutch region.

His next destination was the ancient city of Veraval, and the great ruins of Patan Somnath, which had been destroyed and rebuilt seven times.

Swamiji also visited the new Somnath Temple built by Rani Ahalyabai of Indore, and he bathed at the confluence of the mythological Saraswati, Hiranya and Kapila rivers. Sometime soon after, Swamiji visited another ancient city that of Sudamapuri near Porbandar. Here, he was the guest of Pandit Shankar Pandurang, the *Dewan* and administrator of Porbandar and a great Vedic scholar, who was during that time translating the Vedas. At the insistence of Pandit Pandurang, Swamiji stayed back for some days at Porbandar and helped him with his book. It was during his stay here that Swamiji met another brother-disciple Trigunatitananda precisely in the same manner as he had met Abhedananda. While at Porbandar, Swamiji finished reading Panini's *Mahabhashya*, and learnt French at the insistence of the Pandit. The Pandit told Swamiji to go to the West where 'people will understand you and your worth'.

It was around this time that Swamiji started thinking of visiting the West. He was very much disturbed at the degradation of the glorious ancient culture of the country by the stupid activities and dichotomous lives of its so-called leaders who preached reforms but did not practise it, and, blinded by the glare of the foreign rulers, were trying to supress the age old experiences of the native culture. He therefore felt that in order to enable the civilised world to have a truer picture of India, he must first reach out to them. He had become terribly restless to bring about a spiritual regeneration in India.

The next destination was Dwarka, a city resplendent with legends of Lord Krishna. There, he put up at the Sarada *Math*, the monastery founded by the Shankaracharya. The ruins at Dwarka saddened Swamiji a lot. On his itinerary, the next stop was Mandvi in Kutch, where he visited Narayan Sarovar and Ashapuri.

When parting with Swamiji, his brother-disciple Akhandananda had told him that, whenever he would feel the urge to meet Swamiji, he would travel even if it were to the ends of the world, and seek him out. True to his word, Swamiji's 'Ganges' followed his trail from Jaipur and finally caught up with him at Mandvi and insisted on staying with him. But after Swamiji made him understand that he had to go alone on his mission, he relented and said, 'I had a great longing to see you, and now I am satisfied. Now you can go alone'.

From here, Swamiji moved on to Palitana, where the holy mountain Shatrunjaya — sacred to the Jains and the Muslims alike — is situated. From Palitana he moved to Nadiad, where he stayed at the ancestral house of *Dewan* Haridas Viharidas Desai of Junagadh. There he spent most of his time in the *Dewan*'s library, where he was thrilled to see some excellent paintings by Raja Ravi Varma. Swamiji's next stop was Baroda, the capital of the Gaekwads, where he put up at the residence of a minister of the State. On coming to know that the Prince of Limbdi was at Mahabaleswar, Swamiji immediately left for Mahabaleswar, where he stayed with the Thakore Sahib for about two and a half-months. Next, Swamiji moved on to Poona carrying

Thakore Sahib's recommendations with him and from there he went to Khandwa sometime towards the end of June 1892.

At Khandwa, Swamiji was a guest at the residence of Babu Haridas Chatterjee, a pleader in Khandwa of Bengali origin. Swamiji stayed here for about three weeks and then moved on to Indore, and from there returned to Khandwa once again. This time he was acquainted with one Akshay Kumar Ghosh, who was later adopted by an English lady, Miss Müller, and was subsequently instrumental in Swamiji's visit to England from America in October 1894. It was also at Khandwa that Swamiji first expressed his desire to attend the World Parliament of Religions at Chicago, about which he had first heard at Kathiawar.

Swamiji left Khandwa for Bombay sometime in July that year and was introduced to Seth Ramdas Chhabildas, a noted barrister of Bombay, who later travelled to Chicago with him. It was at Bombay that Swamiji came to know that the educated section of Bengal had opposed the Age of Consent Bill, and was very much pained to hear so. On the positive side, during his stay at Bombay, Swamiji visited the 109 Buddhist caves of Kanheri situated some twenty miles north of the city. This visit stirred him deeply as he felt that he had lived here in a previous life.

He stayed in Bombay for about two months, and then left for Poona. As fate would have it, Lokmanya Bal Gangadhar Tilak was travelling in the same car, and those who had come to see off Swamiji, introduced Tilak to him. Swamiji stayed at Tilak's place in Poona for about ten days, during which time he visited the Deccan Club with Tilak and gave an impromptu philosophical discourse which revealed to everyone present

there his depth of knowledge on the subject. After this incident, people came to him in large numbers to know more about the *Gita* and the *Upanishads*.

Swamiji next moved on to Kolhapur. He gave the local Maharaja the introductory letter that had been given to him by the Maharaja of Bhavnagar. The Maharani of Kolhapur became a devotee of Swamiji and was able to persuade him to accept a new ochre cloth. After a short stay there, Swamiji moved southwards and reached Belgaum around 15th October 1892.

At Belgaum, Swamiji was the guest of a Maharashtrian gentleman who knew the private secretary of the Maharaja of Kolhapur. From the records of Prof. G. S. Bhate — the son of his host at Belgaum — it is found that the non-conforming flesh-eating Hindu monk, who had a deep grounding in Sanskrit scriptures, initially upset his hosts. However, they soon discovered his extraordinary personality which as usual endeared him to the local gentility. The sub divisional forest officer of Belgaum was a Bengali gentleman named Haripada Mitra who was also highly enamoured by Swamiji's preaching and wanted him to come immediately and stay with him. But Swamiji declined to leave the hospitality of the Maharashtrian family, and assured him that he shall do so later. Eventually, he stayed with Haripada Babu for about nine days. Swamiji also told him about his desire to go to America, but not before he completed his vow to visit Rameswaram. At their persistence, both Haripada Babu and his wife were initiated by Swamiji.

From Belgaum, Swamiji reached Goa, which was then a

*Lokmanya Bal Gangadhar Tilak.
(opp.): Dwarka.*

Portuguese colony. Here he adopted the name Sachchidanand. The news of his arrival at Margao preceded him, and he was taken in a procession to the house of his host Subrai Naik, a learned gentleman and friend of Dr. V.V. Shirgaonkar of Belgaum. The main object of Swamiji's visit to Goa was to study Christian theology from old Latin texts and manuscripts which in India were available in Goa alone. Subrai Naik introduced Swamiji to a learned Christian friend of his, J.P. Alvares, who made immediate arrangements for Swamiji's stay at the Rachol Seminary. Here rare religious literature in Latin, both in the form of manuscripts manuscripts and print were kept. Swamiji stayed at the Seminary for three days, and his diligence and grasp of the subject got him friends from the Church as well. Subrai Naik became an ardent follower of Swamiji, and later on even took *sanyas* and became Swami Subramanayanand Tirtha. The room in Subra Naik's house, where Swamiji lived, is still preserved in Vivekananda's memory by Naik's descendants.

Swamiji left Margao by train for Bangalore, via Dharwar, where he was the guest of Dr. P. Palpu, the Medical Officer of the Bangalore Municipality, and a member of the Ezhava community of Kerala. During those days, the higher caste Hindus of the South badly discriminated against the communities belonging to the lower castes and even deprived them of government jobs in spite of their having the necessary qualifications. Swamiji sympathised with their cause and advised them to stop going after the Brahmins and instead, find a noble person from among their own people and emulate him. Dr. Palpu, himself a victim of caste discrimination in his native state of Travancore, took Swamiji's advice seriously and discovered such a person in Shri Narayan Guru, who later on became well known as the leader and guide of the Ezhava community.

At Mysore, Swamiji was initially the guest of Shri K. Seshadri Iyer, the *Dewan* of the Mysore State.

At his residence, Swamiji met many officials and nobles of the Mysore King's Court, who were all impressed with the knowledge and insight of Swamiji. The *Dewan* was sure that his Maharaja, Shri Chamarajendra Wadiyar would be delighted to meet Swamiji, and accordingly, took the 'young *Acharya*' to the Maharaja. The Maharaja was won over by 'such brilliancy of thought, such charm of personality, such wide learning and such penetrating religious insight.' He made Swamiji a state guest and allotted him an apartment in the palace itself.

In Mysore, Swamiji also influenced a Muslim councillor of the State, Abdul Rahman Sahib, who found Swamiji knowledgeable in the Muslim scriptures too and came to him to clear some of his doubts concerning the Koran. Swamiji also amazed everyone with his knowledge of western music,

Sri Chamaraja Wodeyar, Maharaja of Mysore.

which was revealed in his discussions with an Austrian musician at the palace, as he did with his knowledge in electricity, which came out in his discussions with the person entrusted with the installation of electricity in the palace. One day he was invited by the Prime Minister to attend an assembly of *pundits* at the palace hall in Bangalore. His ideas on *Vedanta* enlightened all present and all of them were deeply moved by Swamiji*'s* originality, perception, and treatment of the subject.

One day the Maharaja asked, 'Swamiji, what can I do for you?' Swamiji told him his mission to improve the lot of the Indian people and, in that context, his intention to go to America to preach the philosophical and spiritual sovereignty of India to the westerners, and also to seek from them the means to educate Indians in modern agriculture, industries and other technical sciences. The Maharaja was thoroughly impressed with Swamiji's mission and vision and immediately promised to sponsor his travel to the West. However, Swamiji declined to instantaneously accept the Maharaja's offer, but from that day the Maharaja and his Prime Minister became great admirers of Swamiji.

The Maharaja became greatly attached to Swamiji and was very much distressed when the latter wished to take leave of him. As a remembrance of Swamiji's visit to Mysore, the Maharaja took Swamiji's permission to record his voice on a phonographic record, which, till date, is preserved in the palace museum, although it has since long become indistinct. The Maharaja also wanted to load Swamiji with costly parting gifts, but Swamiji only took a rosewood pipe from him as a memento.

With the railway ticket that the prime minister had bought for him, Swamiji left for Shornur, the gateway to Trichur, and travelled the last twenty-one miles to Trichur by bullock cart. From Trichur, Swamiji moved on to the state of Kodungalloor, famous for its Kali temple, and also a seat of Sanskrit learning. Here, Swamiji himself became a victim of casteism, and, despite his ochre clothes, was not allowed to enter the temple. However, Swamiji's depth in religious matters and his mastery of the Sanskrit language soon found the princes and the princesses of the state seeking guidance from him under a banyan tree near the Kali temple.

From Kodungalloor, Swamiji went to Ernakulam, the capital of the Kochi State, where he met Chattambi Swamikal, the guru of Narayana Guru. Both of them came to appreciate each other's viewpoints, and although both Chattambi Swamikal and Narayana Guru disapproved of Swamiji's meat eating, Chhatambi Swamikal was greatly enamoured by Swamiji's voice. At Ernakulam, Swamiji was the guest of the *Dewan* of Kochi for whom he had a letter of introduction from the Prime Minister of Mysore.

Swamiji left Ernakulam around 6th December 1892 for Thiruvananthapuram, the capital of the state of Travancore. There Swamiji stayed with Prof. Sundaram Iyer, the tutor of the nephew of the Maharaja of Travancore, who was studying for his M.A. degree. The professor was so impressed by Swamiji's personality, his manner of speech, and his discourse on Sri Ramakrishna, that he excused himself that day from his duty at the Palace, and instead, took Swamiji to meet Prof. Rangacharya, a teacher of chemistry at the Trivandrum College with a reputation as a scholar and a man of science.

Swamiji's keen observations of all that happened around him, his gentle manners and sweet temper, his presence of mind and the power of his retort in silencing an opponent, all endeared him to the elite of the city.

On his visit to Prince Martanda Varma, the pupil of his host, Swamiji narrated to him stories of his visits to the courts of various princes during his travel throughout India. He spoke highly of the Rajput chief of Khetri, and the Gaekwad of Baroda, and the ruler of Bangalore, but complained of the generally deteriorating character and capacity of the princes and rulers of the South. Swamiji also met the Maharaja of Travancore, but was not much impressed by his disposition. However, he was earnestly interested in Prince Martanda's studies, and the prince was also very much attracted to Swamiji and even took a photograph of Swamiji which he later sent as an exhibit to the Fine Arts Exhibition held at the Madras Museum.

In his various discourses at Thiruvananthapuram, Swamiji attacked the extravagant claims of people who thought that science has already unravelled the secrets of the universe. He propounded that science itself was in the midst of an evolutionary stage and was still far from understanding the subtle and secret workings of the human mind and its cravings for the realisation of the existence of the One, all else being its limitations and manifestations under the bondage of matter. Swamiji also explained the distinction between gross matter, or *laukik*, and 'fine matter', or *a-laukik*, and how both kept man within the bondage of the senses, and how only those who could overcome such bondages could raise themselves above the petty vanities of the world. Swamiji also delved on casteism and held that the utility of the Brahman would only continue as long as he was unselfish in giving his knowledge freely to the rest of the population. Speaking on women, Swamiji felt that they must receive education from the holy scriptures, imbibe the ancient spiritual culture, and practice the spiritual ideals of the *rishis*. Armed thus with the knowledge of the truths of religion and enlightened perceptions of their needs and requirements, they would then be able to solve their problems themselves. In his discussions with various scholars and other knowledgeable persons, Swamiji would traverse from Spencer to Shakespeare and Kalidas, from Darwin's Theory of Evolution to Jewish History, from Aryan civilisation to the *Vedas*, and from Islam to Christianity. He would say that of all living beings, 'man alone has a hunger in his heart to know the whence and whither, the whys and wherefores of things.'

Some people are of the opinion that it was Swamiji's advise to Dr. Palpu in Bangalore of discovering someone from his own people as a leader that inspired and led to the silent social revolution in Kerala which emphasised on improvement through education and other socially elevating means. Swamiji's rousing call to all classes of the Indian people — made in South India in 1897 after his return from the West — goes to strengthen this viewpoint.

At Thiruvananthapuram, Swamiji searched out his old friend Manmatha Nath Bhattacharya, who was then working as assistant to the accountant general at Madras, and posted in Thiruvananthapuram. Thereafter the two would regularly spend the mornings together. The two friends left for Rameswaram on 22nd December 1892. Enroute, they reached Kanyakumari where Swamiji is said to have meditated on the rocks, now known as the Vivekananda Rocks. He also performed the 'Kumari Puja' by worshipping the 'Mother of the Universe' in the form of Manmatha *babu's* little daughter.

Two rocks, one larger than the other, are situated about two furlongs away from the tip of the mainland into the ocean. According to the *Puranas*, the Divine Mother had appeared on the larger, and farther of these two rocks, when she set her feet there as Devi Kanya to perform *tapasya* to win the hand of Lord Shiva. Hence the *Shaktas*, or worshippers of *Shakti* in the form of the Divine Mother, consider the place highly favourable for spiritual practices. Thus, Swamiji also wanted to go to this rock for his meditation; but there was no boatman in sight. So he plunged into the sea and swam across. His meditation is said to have lasted for three days, during which he had a vision of the greatness and weaknesses that characterized his India. He recognised that it was not religion that brought about the downfall of India, but rather the diversions in the practice thereof, and realised that his country 'shall rise only through a renewal and restoration of that highest spiritual consciousness that has made her the cradle of the nations, and the cradle of the Faith', that is, through the reinstatement of the culture of the *rishis*. The dominance of the priestly classes, the despotic caste system and the divisions that it created in the social body making majority of its followers outcasts, were the insurmountable barriers to the progress of the Indian nation. Vivekananda understood that to remedy the situation, the men of renunciation have to uphold the cause of the Indian downtrodden. He also realised that in India one had to reach out to the masses and not wait for them to come to him. But he found himself helpless, and was plunged into despair. Then suddenly a ray of light shot across the ocean and he found it to be indicative of his Master's direction to proceed to America to earn money by the power of his brain in order to help the Indian multitude.

However, Swamiji was yet to complete his pilgrimage to Rameswaram. He therefore left Kanyakumari to go to Rameswaram and stopped at

(inset): Mother Kumari at Kanya Kumari Temple.

Vivekananda Rock, Kanya Kumari, (extreme left) where he meditated and spent a night during Christmas week in 1892. A memorial now adorns the rock.

Madurai on the way. There he met Bhaskara Setupati, the Raja of Ramnad and an enlightened ruler. The Prince became an admirer and disciple of Swamiji and prodded him to avail of the opportunity that the Parliament of Religions at Chicago offered him and draw the attention of the

Temple at Rameshwaram.

world to Indian spiritual thought. But being eager to visit Rameswaram first, Swamiji took leave of him assuring him that he would soon let him know his decision of going to America.

Rameswaram is immortalised in Ramayana as the place from where Hanuman and his monkey brigade bridged the strait between India and Lanka, now Sri Lanka, where Ravana had held Sita captive. Recent specialised photographs taken by NASA do indicate the existence of such a bridge. It is said that after winning the war with Ravana and rescuing Sita from Sri Lanka, Sri Rama set up a *Shiva-lingam* at Rameswaram, around which is built the present day temple of Rameswaram. Swami Vivekananda had all along cherished a desire to pay his obeisance to Lord Shiva at this temple. Thus reaching Rameswaram was the culmination of his pilgrimage through India. Of the four *dhams*, that is, the four sacred places at virtually the four corners of India, Swamiji visited Dwarka in the west and Rameswaram

in the south, but failed to reach Badrinath in the north as the road to the temple was at that time closed by the Government, and never went to Puri in the east.

The life of a *parivrajaka*, or wandering monk, unfolds not only the character of the places that is visited, but also a multitude of characters that would have otherwise remained uninitiated. The sweetmeat shop owner, who had a dream in which Ram directed him to take food to the hungry Swamiji at Tari Ghat station, was indeed the manifestation of a holy soul. The low caste poor man, who observed Vivekananda talk continuously to the never ending stream of visitors for three consecutive days without food or drink, and then very shakily agreed to cook food for the Swami after a lot of persuasion, could not have been a lesser devotee of Swamiji than his sovereign, the Maharaja of Khetri. His own realisation of the soul being the centre of power — and hence bodily senses of even extreme exhaustions unable to bog down the movement of a *parivrajaka* — was as much an illumination from within, as the eternity of the soul — 'no fear nor death, never was I born, never did I die.' This was as unique an experience as the polyandrous Tibetan countering Swamiji's denunciation of the system with his simple and sincere, albeit faulty, belief that brothers should not have any exclusive possessions and should share everything amongst themselves, even their wives.

Swamiji reached Madras, via Pondicherry, sometime towards the beginning of 1893, and was the guest of his friend Manmathanath. At Pondicherry, he came across a *pandit* from the old school who was vehemently against any idea of Hinduism requiring any sort of reform and considered that contact with the West would pervert the Hindu people. He considered the black waters of the seas as the great dividing line between the land of the Hindus and the lands of the *mlechchhas* or the outcasts, and should therefore never be transgressed.

Manmathanath had organised a handful of Madras's finest young men to welcome Swami Vivekananda at the railway station. Many progressive young men appreciated the ideas of Hinduism as laid down by this new exponent of Hinduism. Madras gave him recognition, and it was his young admirers here who collected the major portion of the funds to enable him to go to America. In Madras he also found people who tuned in to the teachings of his Master, and again, it was his disciples from here who, spread his message even before his return from the West. Madras was also the city where he first started his organisational and publication work.

One of the first to meet Vivekananda at Madras was G.G. Narasimhachari, a member of the Triplicane Literary Society, Madras, who was completely won over by the vastness of Swamiji's knowledge. He found educated men of all ranks and position gathering at Swamiji's place to listen to his enthralling discourses on any and all matters. C. Ramanujachari was one such young man who was dazzled by his knowledge and wit, and later devoted his life to work for the mission in Madras. Swamiji's speeches first attracted young men who found in him a remarkable speaker. But the elders also perceived the depth of knowledge in his speeches, and Swamiji's worth was soon recognised by all and sundry. Swamiji's scientific interpretation of the *Vedas* and his personal touches to the *Vedanta* drew both adoration and aplomb.

Amongst Vivekananda's admirers in Madras were Kamakshi Natarajan, one of the most powerful Indian journalists of that time, and *Dewan* Bahadur Raghunath Rao, a national figure and author of several legal treatises. It was a discourse of Swamiji, where he dealt upon the western interpretation of eastern culture, that impressed these two stalwarts of the time, and a decision to send Swamiji to the Chicago Congress was taken soon after that. Another one of Vivekananda's admirers was Singaravelu Mudaliar, the assistant professor of science at the Christian College, an atheist who also appreciated the practical values of Christianity. He had come to argue with Swamiji, but, after speaking with him, became his devoted disciple, and was later on the honorary manager of *Prabuddha Bharat*, the publication that Swamiji started in Madras after his return from the West. Then there was V. Subramanya Iyer who joined his college friends on their visit to Swamiji 'to have fun', but was won over when Swamiji put his friends to place in their own game. Thereafter, Iyer used to accompany Swamiji daily on his evening walks, and it was during one such walk that Swamiji asked him, 'Well, my boy, can you wrestle?' and on receiving an answer in the affirmative, continued, 'Come, let us have a tussle.' It was this athletic streak

of Vivekananda that made Iyer call him the *Pahalwan Swami*, or the athlete Swami.

Thus, his holding equal ground in wrestling and fencing as in discussions pertaining to the Universal Soul brought him nearer to the people of Madras. They found that Swamiji was down to earth and was not afraid of indulging in fun and frolic also. But it was his undaunted patriotism that endeared him the most. They found that the young monk, who had renounced everything, was obsessed with his love for the country and was thus grief stricken with its downfall. He would say, 'Can you adduce any reason why India should lie in the ebb-tide of the Aryan nations? Is she inferior in intellect? Is she inferior in dexterity? Can you look at her art, at her mathematics, at her philosophy, and answer yes? All that is needed is that she should de-hypnotise herself and wake up from her age-long sleep to take her true rank in the hierarchy of nations.'

The hopes of the people of Madras in Swami Vivekananda were not aroused by what Sri Ramakrishna had said about him, but emanated from their personal association with him. While many of them found him imbibed with the spirit of the Holy Scriptures, others discerned in him a master of the philosophical and scientific outlook of the West. As one of his disciples wrote, 'From the *Rig Veda* to *Ramayana*, from *Vedanta* philosophy to Kant and Hegel, the whole range of ancient and modern literature and art and music, from the sublimes of ancient yoga to the intricacies of a modern laboratory, everything seemed clear to his field of vision.'

Vivekananda had long cherished the idea of attending the World Parliament of Religions to be held at Chicago. He announced his intention to all those he knew in Madras. As a result, some of them started collecting money for his proposed travel. But Swamiji had still not found a clear indication of the 'Mother' in the matter, and thus asked his disciples to distribute the collected money among the poor. Swamiji was now in a devotional state of mind and almost continuously prayed to the 'Mother' and his Master for direction, and meditated intensely.

It was around this time that the people of Hyderabad, who had heard about Vivekananda from their friends in Madras, begged him to come to Hyderabad for at least a brief visit. Manmathanath telegraphed his friend, Madhusudan Chatterjee, the superintendent engineer to His Highness the Nizam of Hyderabad, informing him that Swamiji would be reaching Hyderabad on 10th February 1893. On his arrival at Hyderabad, the people of the twin cities of Hyderabad and Secunderabad gave him a rousing welcome. A motley crowd, led by some very distinguished members of the Royal Court, several from the nobility and many pandits, pleaders and merchants gathered at the railway station to welcome him. It was a magnificent reception, befitting a prince.

The next morning, Vivekananda went to visit the Golconda Fort. When he returned, he found Khurshid Jha, K.C.S.I, the private secretary of the Nawab's brother-in-law, waiting for him with an invitation to visit the palace the following morning. Accordingly, Swamiji went to the palace on the scheduled date and had discussions on Hinduism, Christianity and Islam. On the Nawab's taking exception to the idea of Personal God as presented in Hinduism, Swamiji explained that the concept of 'Him' as a Person was necessitated by human experience being personal in nature and thus the highest that the human thought could rise had to be personal. He went on to say that other than Hinduism all other religions have been founded by some person or the other, and that only the *Vedanta* is based on eternal principles and thus could claim to be Universal. The Nawab was highly pleased with Vivekananda's understanding of the religions, and, on coming to know of his intention to attend the Chicago summit, he immediately offered a purse of a thousand rupees. But Swamiji told the Nawab of his waiting for the 'command', and assured him that he will let him know as soon as he receives it.

The following morning, he met the prime minister and some other nobles of the state, and all of them offered to support his proposed visit to America. In the afternoon he spoke on *My Mission to the West* at the Mahboob College, where more than a thousand people, including many Europeans, attended the pre-arranged lecture. His command over the English language, his eloquence, his learning and his power of exposition endeared him to all present there, and the very next day the bankers of the Begum Bazar promised to help him with his passage money.

Vivekananda's pious simplicity, unfailing self-control and profound meditation made an indelible impression on the citizens of Hyderabad, and on 17th February 1893, when he was leaving for Madras — there were more than a thousand people who came to see him off at the railway station. At Madras also, Swamiji was given a warm welcome by his disciples.

Each day brought new disciples and devotees, and constant and combined persuasion from them made Swamiji ponder over the idea of going to America. He finally agreed to the formation of a subscription committee headed by devoted follower, Alasinga Perumal. Swamiji, however, wanted his devotees to collect subscriptions only from the masses so that he could get an indication of the Mother's will in the matter. People gave money not only out of their devotion towards him, but also from their conviction that he was destined to accomplish his mission there.

By mid April enough money had been collected. But, although Swamiji saw the signs of his Mother's will in the readiness of his disciples, and the collection of the required money from the people, he wanted direct command from his Master. He continued praying to the Mother and

Master for guidance. One night, as he lay half asleep, the command came to him in a dream. He saw his Master walking from the seashore into the waters of the ocean and beckoning him to follow. Vivekananda understood the divine command in that vision, and all his doubts vanished. But a bad dream concerning his mother's health disturbed his peace of mind and he wanted to know the reality badly before leaving for America. However, in order to remain untraceable, Swamiji was not corresponding with anyone in Calcutta, so he asked his friend Manmathanath to get the news somehow. Manmathanath sent a telegram to Calcutta, the reply whereof brought good news about his mother. Thus, one more important obstacle was also cleared.

In the meantime, Vivekananda spoke at least twice at the Theosophical Society in Madras, and his versatility in western philosophy and modern science enchanted the audience there. But when Swamiji declined to join the society, the then leader of the society, an American named Colonel Olcott, refused to give him even a letter of introduction to anyone in America.

The Mother's final dictat came in the form of a reply from the Holy Mother, Sarada Devi, who was elated to receive her Naren's letter after so long. She wrote back giving her blessings to his mission, which she knew was the wish of the Master. On receiving the Holy Mother's letter, Swamiji wept with joy, and proclaimed, 'Let us go to work in right earnest. The Mother Herself has spoken.'

When all arrangements for Vivekananda's sailing from Madras to America were complete, Munshi Jagmohanlal, the private secretary to the Raja of Khetri arrived in Madras to request Swamiji to come with him for the celebration of the birth of a son to the Raja, who had been blessed by the Swami during his earlier visit to the kingdom. Jagmohanlal prostrated before the Swami and pleaded with him to come to Khetri at least for a day to bless the child. Although Swamiji tried to

The Holy Mother, Sri Sarada Devi (1853-1920).

break free of the situation, he finally gave in to Jagmohanlal's constant pleadings, and it was decided that he would now sail from Bombay.

Swamiji's Madras disciples bade him a touching farewell, and he left for Khetri via Bombay. At Bombay, he unexpectedly came across Haribhai (Swami Turiyananda) and Rakhal (Swami Brahmananda) who had come there from Karachi in the course of their pilgrimage. Swamiji disclosed his plans to go to America to Swami Turiyananda. After staying for a few days at Bombay, he and Jagmohanlal left for Khetri.

Khetri was all decked up for the festivities that were going on to celebrate the birth of a son to their king. But the Raja was all humility and prostrated himself before Swamiji in full view of his state guests comprising of many princes and chiefs of Rajputana. All those present rose to their feet and the Raja introduced Swamiji to the assembled guests. On coming to know of his intention to visit the West to preach the doctrines of the *Sanatana Dharma*, the celebrity gathering applauded heartily. Then the little prince was brought in to be blessed by the Swami.

The Swami stayed in Khetri for almost three weeks, and then left for Bombay on 10th May to make preparations for his voyage to America. Jagmohan accompanied him till Bombay and saw to his every need for the voyage. It was also at the request of the Raja of Khetri that Swamiji reassumed the name of Vivekananda for good, leaving behind the name Sachchhidanand that he had been using in the South. En route to Bombay, he again met Haribhai and Rakhal at the Abu Road station. They had come from Mount Abu to meet him. Swamiji directed Turiyananda to leave for the *Math* immediately to 'do the Master's work there and try for the improvement of the *Math*.'

Swamiji had written to his Madras disciples confirming his intention to board the ship at Bombay, and not Madras. Alasinga Perumal reached Bombay in time to receive him. Jagmohan was instructed by his Raja to deck up Vivekananda for the Religious Parliament, and, accordingly, he took the Swami to the best shops in Bombay and got prepared for him robes and turbans of silk and suiting. Swamiji's objections fell on deaf ears, and Jagmohan even got a first-class steamer ticket for him.

On 31st May 1893, Swamiji boarded the steamer *Peninsular*. He was dressed in a silken robe and turban, and the farewells, and the uncertainties and formalities of foreign travel bogged him down as much as the many belongings that he had to care for. He stood on the deck of the ship as long as the motherland was visible to him, and sent out his blessings to all those who loved him and all whom he loved. His eyes filled with tears, and he was overwhelmed with emotions as he thought of the Master, of the Holy Mother, of his brother-disciples, of India and her culture, of her greatness and her sufferings, of the *rishis* and of *Sanatana Dharma*.

During his travels across the length and breadth of India, Vivekananda had realised the essence of Jainism and Buddhism, the spirit of Ramanand and Dayanand, and had become a great *bhakta* of Tulsidas and Nischaldas. He had learnt about the saints of Maharashtra, Alwar and southern India, and also understood the hopes and aspirations of the *bhangis* and the downtrodden. He was deeply touched by the widespread ignorance, misery and squalor of the common Indian and felt a 'fierce desire to change such evil conditions.' He sincerely believed in the *karma* of relieving the sufferings of his countrymen and reaching God through service to the starving multitudes. He replied to the criticism of his choosing to stay mainly with princes and their d*ewans* by saying 'If I can win over to my cause those in whose power are wealth and the administration of the affairs of thousands, my mission will be accomplished sooner; by influencing one Maharaja alone I can indirectly benefit thousands of people.'

Vivekananda understood the unifying ethos of all masterpieces, and found in Shahjahan's Taj Mahal the same pathos as in Kalidasa's *Shakuntala*. He sang the songs of Mirabai and Tansen with the same verve as he sang those of Guru Nanak, and he cited the stories of Delhi's Prithvi Raj Chauhan and Chittor's Rana Pratap with the same gusto as he did those of Shiva and Uma, Krishna and Radha, and Ram and Sita. His whole heart and soul was the burning epic of India, and his great mind could visualise a connection where others only saw isolated facts. His mind pierced the soul of things and presented facts in their real order. His was the most universal mind, with a perfect practical culture, and he was the one who realised that 'India will be raised not with the power of the flesh, but with the power of spirit; not with the flag of destruction, but with the flag of peace and love.' Thus, he was the perfect representative of India at the Chicago conference.

The journey by ship was altogether a new experience for Swami Vivekananda, but the mighty expanse of the ocean, the invigorating air, the carefree atmosphere, and the courteous behaviour of all aboard helped him gradually reconcile himself to this new life. He soon acclimatised himself with the unfamiliar food, the strange environment, and the people, and got himself acquainted with the manners and customs of the Europeans.

The first stop of the ship was Colombo, where it was anchored for a day. Swamiji availed of the opportunity to go around the city; the gigantic statue of the reclining Buddha fascinating him the most. The next stop was Penang in the Malay Peninsula, with a predominantly Muslim population and known to have been infested with pirates till not long ago. The next port was Singapore, which was then the capital of the Straits Settlements. Here Swamiji visited the museum and the Botanical Garden. En route Singapore he also caught a glimpse of Sumatra.

Swamiji had his first experience of China at Hong Kong, which was the ship's next stop. Although the very name brought forth the image of a land of dreams and romance, Swamiji found the Chinese people adept in commercial activities. By watching the lifestyle of the boat people in the harbour and the Si-Kiang river, during a boat ride to Canton some eighty miles away, he could easily find a similarity between the Chinese and the Indian, and realised that it was poverty that had bound each of them to mummified civilisations. In Canton, Swamiji visited several Buddhist temples, and was surprised to find that Chinese ladies were as much a victim of the *zenana* system as the North Indian women. With great difficulty, he also managed to visit a Chinese monastery, which were usually considered inaccessible to foreigners.

The ship was anchored in Hong Kong for three days, after which it sailed for Nagasaki in Japan. Swamiji found the Japanese people to be one of the cleanest in the world. He was greatly intrigued by their 'picturesque' lifestyle, and in order to learn more about the country, he disembarked at Kobe and took the land route to Yokohama. En route, he visited the industrial town of Osaka, the former capital Kyoto and the present capital Tokyo. He was enamoured by the penetration of modernism in every sphere of

An early photograph in America.

knowledge and the general awareness of the necessities of the modern times. He visited all the important temples in these three cities, and studied the rituals, ceremonies and customs of the Japanese people. He was surprised to see, that like in China, there were inscriptions of Sanskrit scriptures in old Bengali characters on the inner walls of some of these temples. The only explanation that occurred to him was that some Bengali *bhikkhus*, or Buddhist monks, must have visited there and have taken leading roles to spread Buddhism in these two countries.

On 14th July Swamiji left Yokohama for Vancouver on a bigger ship, the *Empress of India*, and reached British Columbia on the evening of 25th July. From here he took the Canadian Pacific Railway to Chicago. It took him almost five days to reach his destination through Canada and the American states of Minnesota and Wisconsin, and he probably reached Chicago on 30th July 1893. His first experiences at the railway station were not very encouraging, and so, to be on the safe side, he checked into one of the bigger hotels of Chicago.

The Parliament of Religions was still three months away, but the parent international fair, the World's Fair, was already on and all the latest inventions and arts were being exhibited there. Vivekananda marvelled at the exhibits, and more so, at the human minds behind those creations. But Chicago was a big city and quite expensive, and Swamiji knew that his purse would not carry him through the six odd weeks till the Parliament of Religions began. Moreover, he had no references that every delegate to the Conference required to have. Meanwhile, he came to know that Boston was much less expensive, and therefore, after spending twelve days in Chicago, he boarded a train for Boston.

On the train he met a resident of Boston, a lady by the name of Katherine Abbott Sanborn. She was highly impressed by Swamiji and requested him to be her guest at Boston. Sanborn was a lecturer and author and had a good circle of friends. It was through her that Swamiji met Dr. John Henry Wright, a professor of Greek at the Harvard University. Wright invited Swamiji to spend the weekend, that is 26th and 27th August with his family at a small and quiet village resort at Massachusetts on the Atlantic coast where they were vacationing.

The vastly learned Professor was highly impressed by Vivekananda's depth of knowledge and insisted that he represent Hinduism at the Parliament of Religions. When Swamiji told him that he had no credentials with him, the Professor replied, 'To ask you Swami for credentials is like asking the sun to state its right to shine.' The Professor knew many distinguished people associated with the Parliament, and wrote an introductory letter for Swamiji to the Chairman of the Committee for Selection of Delegates, stating, 'Here is a man who is more learned than all our learned professors put together.' He also presented the Swami with the passage money to Chicago, and also him introductory letters for the committee in charge of accommodating and providing for the Oriental delegates.

This was indeed godsend and Swami Vivekananda rejoiced at this Divine indication. But, before returning to Chicago, he spent a busy week at Massachusetts in the house of Kate Tannatt Woods. There, he addressed several gatherings, and spoke about Indian culture, the Hindu dharma and India's needs.

On 4th September, he left Mrs. Woods' residence for Saratoga in New York where he was to speak not once, but thrice at the American Social Science Association, where Franklin Sanborn, the brother of Katherine Sanborn of Boston, was the secretary. It was a rare honour shown to a young unknown Hindu monk.

Vivekananda returned to Chicago around 9th September 1893, but somehow landed in the northeast section where most of the population

consisted of people of German origin. The language gap made him spend the night in a huge empty box in the railway yard. The next morning, he woke up very hungry and went begging for food in the direction of the office of Dr. John Henry Barrows, Chairman of the Parliament's General Committee. But the local people treated him very rudely, and, this made Swamiji lose heart. Exhausted as he was from hunger, he resigned to fate and sat down on the footsteps of a playground. It was then that a lady came out of a house opposite the playground and softly asked him if he was a delegate to the Conference of the World Religions. On his confirming the same, the lady, George W. Hale, took him to her house, where he bathed and had his breakfast. After that, she personally accompanied Swamiji to the office of the Parliament.

Swami Vivekananda was accepted as a delegate, and was assigned lodging at the house of Mr. and Mrs. John B. Lyon at 262, Michigan Avenue. Swamiji passed his time praying and meditating, and in earnest longing that he might be blessed as the true spokesman for Hinduism and true bearer of his Master's message. He also became acquainted with many other delegates to the Parliament.

The Parliament of Religions, an adjunct of the Chicago World's Fair, was held from 11th to 27th September 1893, and it left an indelible mark in the history of religions, especially that of the Hindu religion. Delegates to the Parliament represented every form of organised religious belief, and came from all parts of the world.

The Parliament roused a wave of new awareness in the western world, and specially in America, and as the Honourable Merwin-Marie

Snell, the President of the Scientific Section, put it, 'One of its chief advantages has been in the great lesson which it has taught the Christian World, especially to the people of the United States, namely that there are other religions more venerable than Christianity and which surpass it in philosophical depth, in spiritual intensity, in independent vigour of thought, and in breadth and sincerity of human sympathy, while not yielding to it a single hair's breadth in ethical beauty and efficiency.'

The Art Institute of Chicago.

(opp.): From left to right: Virchand Gandhi, Hewivitarne Dharmapala and Swami Vivekananda.

There were thousands of delegates at the Parliament, and Swami Vivekananda was the youngest of them all. Eight great non-Christian religious groups were represented: Buddhism, Confucianism, Hinduism, Jainism, Judaism, Mazdaism, Mohammedanism and Shintoism. There were six delegates from India — Swamiji representing Hinduism, Pratap Chandra Mazumdar representing the Brahmo Samaj, Virchand Gandhi representing Jainism, Chakravarti representing the Theosophical Society, and Mrs. Annie Besant and Nagarkar.

The historic and unprecedented Parliament was held in Chicago's newly constructed and imposing Art Institute on the Michigan Avenue. The seventeen day Parliament had amongst the delegates and audience some of the most distinguished and learned people of the world. While the main sessions of the Parliament were held at the Hall of Columbus, the readings of the papers, and addresses of more scientific and less popular character, were delivered either at the adjoining Hall of Washington or the other smaller halls of the building. In addition to his scheduled addresses and impromptu talks at the Columbus Hall, Swami Vivekananda also spoke several times at the Washington Hall.

On the morning of the opening of the Parliament, the delegates assembled at the Art Institute, from where they were taken in a grand procession inside the Hall of Columbus that was packed beyond its capacity. After the initial ceremonies were over, the delegates were introduced one by one and they went up to the podium and spoke. Swami Vivekananda's position in the numerical order was 31, but he requested the President to let him speak the last. His heart was fluttering, and his tongue nearly dried up, and he did not even have a prepared speech with him, but when his turn came, he prayed to *Devi* Saraswati, the goddess of learning and stepped up when Dr. Barrows introduced him; the rest is history.

The moment he addressed the gathering as 'Sisters and Brothers of America', he received a thundering standing ovation that lasted for full two minutes from the seven thousand odd people who had gathered there that day. When silence was restored, he began his short speech by thanking the youngest of nations on behalf of the most ancient order of monks in the world, the Vedic Order of *sanyasis*, and introduced Hinduism as 'the Mother of Religions, a religion which has taught the world both tolerance and universal acceptance.'

The essence of Swamiji's message was *Universal Religion*, and while emphatically declaring that no religion is either superior or inferior to the other, he quoted from the Hindu scriptures and said, 'As the different streams having their sources in different places all mingle their water in the sea, so, O Lord, the different paths which men take, through different tendencies, various though they may appear, crooked or straight, all lead to Thee.' It was a message of Unity in Diversity, and Swamiji disclosed that he had learnt it at the feet of his Master who had taught and practiced that all religions were one, and that they were all paths leading to God.

This was Swamiji's introductory, or welcome speech made on 11th September. Thereafter, he spoke on 15th September on *Why We Disagree*, on 19th September on *Hinduism*, on 20th September on *Religion not the Crying Need of India*, on 26th September on *Buddhism, The Fulfilment of Hinduism*, and finally gave his concluding address at the Final Session on 27th September.

In *Why We Disagree* he compared the believers of the different religions each of whom considered

their religion to the best akin to the frog in a well who imagined that nothing could ever be bigger than his well. He thanked the organisers of the Parliament for their attempt to break down the different wells and for bringing forth the truth. Swamiji spoke about Universal Religion, but accepted that differences will naturally remain in the philosophy, mythology and rituals of different religions. He advocated acceptance of the Truth in whatever forms it is expressed, and recognising human beings as they are.

Swamiji spoke about 'Hinduism' being the only prehistoric religion that is still in practice. Speaking about the other two, he said that while Judaism was driven out by its all-conquering daughter Christianity, whom it had failed to absorb; only a handful of Parsees is all that remains to tell the tale of the grand religion of Zoroastrianism. He reckoned that unlike other existing religions founded by a particular person, the Hindus received their religion through revelation of the eternal *Vedas*, which consisted of the accumulated treasury of spiritual laws discovered by different persons at different times. He indicated that just like the law of gravity existed even before it was actually discovered, the laws governing the spiritual relations between soul and soul, and between individual spirits and the Father of all spirits, had been there even before the various *rishis* discovered them at different times. He said that the Vedic teaching of creation was without either a beginning or an end in the light of the scientific theory that the sum total of cosmic energy is always the same. He stressed on human soul being eternal and immortal, and death meaning only a change of the soul from one body to another. He said that the *Vedas* also teach that the soul is divine and that it is possible for the individual spirit to become one with

Swami Vivekananda and Narasimhacharya.

(opp.): The Parliament of Religions in Chicago.

the Father of all spirits through *mukti*, which can be achieved only through purity. Thus, the whole object of Hinduism is to attain divinity through perfection, to see God and to reach Him. Swamiji compared this with the perfection sought by scientists in their respective sciences.

Sister Nivedita in her introduction to *The Complete Works of Swami Vivekananda*, has very aptly described this address:, 'Of the Swami's address before the Parliament of Religions, it may be said that when he began to speak it was of the religious ideas of the Hindus, but when he ended, Hinduism had been created.'

In *Religion not the Crying Need of India*, Swamiji took the Christians to task for sending missionaries to save the souls of the Indians when what they needed was food to save their bodies from starvation. He said that there was enough religion in the East, and it was bread that they actually needed. He openly declared that he 'came here to seek aid for my impoverished people.'

Speaking about the relationship between 'Hinduism and Buddhism', he compared it with the relationship between Judaism and Christianity but he also reminded the gathering that whereas the Jews not only rejected Jesus Christ but also crucified him, the Hindus accepted Shakya Muni — as Buddha is known to them — in the form of God and worshiped him. But unlike the Jews who did not understand the teachings of Christ, here, it was the Buddhists themselves who did not realise the importance of the teachings of Buddha. He pointed out that the religion of the Hindus is divided into two parts; the ceremonial and the spiritual. But whereas the caste system was prevalent in the ceremonial part — as practiced by the masses — it was absent in the spiritual part as studied by the monks and Shakya Muni was a monk who brought out the hidden truth of the *Vedas* and opened it in front of the world. To the Buddhist everyone was equal, as is also practised by the Hindu monks, but the Buddhists dashed themselves against the eternal foundation of the *Vedas* and tried to take away the eternal God from the people, and the result was the natural death of Buddhism in India, the land of its birth. The fact is that neither Buddhism nor Hinduism can exist without the other thus the separation of the two is the cause of the Indian downfall.

While addressing the Final Session of the Parliament of Religions, Swami Vivekananda thanked the organisers for conceptualising the

Parliament and making it a reality, the delegates for their liberal views, and the audience 'for their uniform kindness to me and for their appreciation of every thought that tends to smooth the friction of religions.' He once again stressed on Unity in Diversity, but advised respect of the diversity of different religions. He compared the spirit that had evolved at the Parliament as the culmination of the implanted seed into a plant with the aid of earth, air and water, without actually becoming any of those three, and stressed on 'Help and not fight', 'Assimilation and not Destruction', and 'Harmony and Peace and not Dissension' as the basis of growth of every religion, which must assimilate the spirit of the others and yet preserve its individuality and grow according to its own law of growth.

Besides speaking on these five days at the Plenary Session of the Parliament, Swamiji also spoke before the Scientific Section and the Universal Religions Unity Congress on matters concerning *Orthodox Hinduism and the Vedanta Philosophy, The Modern Religions of India, The Essence of the Hindu Religion, Women in Oriental Religion, The Love of God* and other topics.

Although it was Swamiji who had wanted to be the very last speaker on the first day, thereafter the organisers sensed his immense popularity with the audience, and used to deliberately keep Swami Vivekananda until the end of the programme to make people stay for the whole session. Such was the spirit and self-confidence of Swami Vivekananda, that despite being in a totally alien environment, he not only spoke eloquently on the topics he chose but also accosted the ignorance of the host nation and some of the other speakers at the Parliament. On one occasion, pausing in the midst of his discourse, he said that all those in the audience who had read the sacred books of the Hindus, and who therefore had first hand knowledge of the Hindu religion, should raise their hands. On finding that there were only three people who did so, the Swami raised himself to his full height, and, in a rebuking voice said, 'And yet you dare to judge us!' Similarly, just before reading his paper on Hinduism, and after the applause was over on his being introduced as the next speaker, Swamiji began by saying, 'We, who have come from the East, have sat here day after day and have been told in a patronising way that we ought to accept Christianity because Christian nations are the most prosperous. We look about us and we see England the most prosperous Christian nation in the world, with her foot on the neck of 25,00,00,000 Asiatic. We look back into history and see that the prosperity of Christian Europe began with Spain and Spain's prosperity began with the invasion of Mexico. Christianity wins its prosperity by cutting the throats of its fellow men. The Hindu will not have prosperity at such a price. I have sat here today and I have heard the height of intolerance. Blood and the sword are not for the Hindu, whose religion is based on the law of love.'

The press was most eloquent about Swami Vivekananda and even well-known periodicals of the day quoted his speeches in full. Even the most rigid and orthodox Christians would also say, 'He is indeed a prince among men.' His fellow country person, and co-speaker at the Parliament, Annie Besant's first impression of Swamiji was 'Shining like the sun of India in the midst of the heavy atmosphere of Chicago...' and instead of elaborating on 'that matchless evangel of the East', she quoted what she overheard a member of the audience remarking, when he came out of the Columbus Hall after listening to Swami Vivekananda, 'That man a heathen? And we send missionaries to his people! It would be more fitting that they should send missionaries to us.' So meteoric was the transformation of Swami Vivekananda from obscurity to fame, that it can truly be said that he 'awoke one morning to find himself famous'.

Although the Indian press had been reporting the proceedings of the Parliament of Religions and

SWAMI VIVE KANANDA

·The Hindoo Monk of India·

Poster of Swamiji during the Parliament of Religions.

about Swami Vivekananda since September itself, it was only after a reprint of the 23rd September *Boston Evening Transcript* entitled 'Hindus at the Fair' in the leading papers of the three presidencies in November, that the news made an impact on the Indian people at large. Thereafter, the American reports of Swami Vivekananda's success were reprinted regularly in the leading Indian newspapers, notably the *Indian Mirror*.

Swami Vivekananda's performance at the Parliament of Religions made him famous throughout the world, but name and fame did not affect him, and he remained the *sanyasi* with a burning desire to change the future of the poor Indians. Thus began his mission in its public aspect, and although the ascetic life of the wandering monk was over, the days of intense thought and work began.

After the Parliament of Religions, the Slayton Lyceum Lecture Bureau signed him up, and from the fall of 1893 to the end of 1894 he toured eastern America. He also got invited as far north as Canada and to Memphis in the south. At times, Swamiji gave up to fourteen lectures a week, inclusive of class talks and parlour talks, and not all of these were on religion. Towards the beginning of 1895, he took an apartment in New York City and began weekly classes and discourses on *Yoga*.

Swamiji observed that the billions of people on the earth could be classified into four basic types — those who were in constant activity, or the worker; those who were driven by their inner urge to achieve something in life, or the lover; those who tended to analyse the working of their minds, and work with their minds, or the mystic; and those who weighed everything with reason, or the philosopher. He found that each of the four different forms of *Yoga* of the Vedantic Vision of Universal Religion could help each of these four kinds of people. Each of these individuals lay stress on some value or the other which highlight the impact of their actions on their surroundings, and 'to the active worker it is the union between individuals and humanity as such; to the lover, union between himself and the God of love; to the mystic, between his lower 'self' and higher 'self'; and to the philosopher it is the union of all existence'. Swami Vivekananda recommended *Karma Yoga* for the worker, *Bhakti Yoga* for the lover, *Raja Yoga* for the mystic and *Gyan Yoga* for the philosopher.

KARMA YOGA

The word *Karma* is derived from the Sanskrit *'Kri'*, to do. All action is *karma*, and technically this word also encompasses the effects of actions. But *karma yoga* deals only with *karma* as work, without its effects.

According to eastern philosophy, the goal of mankind is knowledge, and miseries are caused when men foolishly strive to attain pleasure instead. Pleasure and pain are good teachers, and so are good and evil, and all these go to build the character of a man.

Knowledge is inherent in man, and learning is discovering or unveiling the cover of one's own soul, which is a mine of infinite knowledge. The external world is simply the suggestion that sets one to study one's own mind, the object of study being the mind itself. The falling of an apple gave the suggestion to Newton, and he studied his own mind; he rearranged all the previous links of thought in his mind and discovered a new link among them, which he termed as gravity. Like fire in the flint, knowledge exists in the mind; a suggestion is the friction igniting it.

In many cases knowledge is not discovered, and different stages of learning depend on the advancement in the process of discovering one's 'learning'. The man who is unable to lift the veil and discover is an ignorant man, the man who has been able to lift it to a certain degree is knowledgeable, and the man who has removed the veil totally is all knowing, omniscient.

Every mental and physical perception by the mind leading to the discovery of some or the other knowledge is *karma*. Everything we do, physical or mental, is *karma*, and it leaves its mark on us. The effect of *karma* on one's character is the most tremendous power that man has to deal with. Great occasions rouse even the lowest of human beings to some kind of greatness, but a real great man continues doing even the most common actions in the same way always and wherever he may be.

Swamiji added that our *karma* determines what we deserve and what we can assimilate. We are responsible for what we are, and we have the power to make ourselves whatever we wish to. If what we are now has been the result of our own past actions, it certainly follows that whatever we wish to be in future can be produced by our present actions, and *Karma Yoga* shows us how to act now to achieve what we want to be.

The *Gita* describes *Karma Yoga* as doing work with cleverness and scientifically to bring out the inherent power of the mind, and to awaken the soul. 'To work we have the right, but not to the fruits thereof'. If one wants to do a great or a good work, one need not bother about what the result will be. Intense activity is necessary and one must continue working. The ideal man is he who, in the midst of the greatest silence and solitude finds the intensest activity, and in the midst of that activity finds the silence and solitude of the desert. Such a man has learnt the secret of restraint; he has established himself as an ideal *Karma Yogi*.

Different people work with different motives — some work for fame, some for money, some for power, and some want to go to heaven. But there are a few exceptions, those who work for work's sake, those who do not care for name, or fame, or even to go to heaven, and it is from amongst such characters that a Christ or a Buddha is made.

One has to start at the beginning, take up different works as they come to him, and slowly make himself more unselfish with every passing day. We must do the work and find out the motive power that prompts us, and initially, we will find that all our motives are selfish, but gradually this selfishness will melt by persistence, and at last we will reach a time when we shall be able to do work without any selfish motive. We may all hope that someday we will all reach this stage and become perfectly unselfish; and the moment we attain this stage, all our powers will be concentrated, and the knowledge which is ours will manifest.

BHAKTI YOGA

Bhakti is the intense love of God, and *Bhakti Yoga* is search of God, beginning, continuing, and ending in love. When a man is in true love of God, he loves all, hates none, and is always satisfied. This love is beyond worldly desires, and is often the cause of the denunciation of everything else. However, the weak and undeveloped minds of the

worshippers on the lower strata of *Bhakti* are often carried away by the love of their own ideal only and shut themselves from other ideals, which may lead to fanaticism. Swami Vivekananda compared this sort of *Bhakti* to the canine instinct of guarding the master's property from intrusion, and went on to explain that, unlike the fanatic, the dog at least never mistakes its master for an enemy, no matter in what dress the master appears before it.

Bhakti is a succession of mental efforts at religious realisation, beginning with ordinary worship, and ending in a supreme intensity of love of *Ishwar*, 'from whom is the birth, continuation, and dissolution of the universe; the Eternal, the Pure, the Ever-Free, the Almighty, the All-knowing, the All-merciful, the Teacher of all teachers from *The Philosophy of Ishvara* by Swami Vivekananda).

Swamiji stressed that like the bird flying to its destination with the help of its two wings, and steering through by its tail, love of God can be attained through *Gyan* or knowledge, and *Bhakti* or devotion, with *Yoga* maintaining the balance between the two. Neither *Bhakti* nor *Gyan* alone can fetch the desired goal.

Bhakti Yoga is divided into two forms — the *gauna*, also known as *apara*, meaning preparatory; and the *para*, or the supreme. In the preparatory stage, the mythological and symbolical aspects of religion help the aspiring soul become 'God-ward'. This form of *Bhakti Yoga* can, at the most, bring about only the so-called spirit of reform amongst its practitioners to whom enjoyment of their lives is the only purpose of human existence, and the *bhakta* is engrossed in his *Bhakti* alone and considers all other forms irrelevant.

'Every soul is destined to be perfect, and every being, in the end, will attain the state of perfection. Whatever we are now is the result of our acts and thoughts in the past, and whatever we shall be in the future will be the result of what we think and do now.' The *guru*, or the teacher, from whose soul the impulse comes and hastens the higher powers and possibilities of the soul, awakens the spiritual life, nurtures the growth of the *shishya*, or the disciple so that he may become holy and perfect in the end. Whereas the *guru* must possess the power to transmit that impulse, the *shishya* must also be fit to receive it, and then only will the spiritual awakening succeed. A true religious teacher should have a pure soul and possess the knowledge of the 'spirit of the scriptures' more than the mere words of the scriptures, and should be teaching without any motive and out of love alone. The *shishya* on the other hand should be pure of heart, and have a real thirst for knowledge. He should also have perseverance and should love and venerate his teacher.

Purity, strength, control of one's passions, and discrimination are some of the essentials of *Bhakti Yoga*. Truthfulness, sincerity, doing good for others without any gain to one's self, and *ahimsa* or not injuring others by thought, word or deed — are some of the ingredients of purity. The *Bhakti Yogi* must have both mental and physical strength, and be sound in both.

Repeating God's name, and following the rituals and symbols are part of the preparatory form of *Bhakti Yoga*. But a *Yogi* who wants to tread on the path of the supreme form of this *Yoga* will have to renounce the world, and immerse himself completely in the love of God.

However, this renunciation comes naturally to the *Bhakta* out of his intense love of God. *Bhakti Yoga* does not say, 'give up', it only says, 'love, love, love the Highest', and thus it leads to spiritual bliss. It makes the heart fill with the divine waters of the ocean of love, that is God Himself, and leaves no place there for love of anything else.

RAJA YOGA

Raja Yoga is the science evolved through the analysis of the study, investigation and generalisation of the religious faculties of man in its entirety. *Raja Yoga* does not deny the existence of unexplained facts, rather it asserts that miracles, and answers to prayers do not become comprehensible through superstitious explanations or by attributing them to supernatural beings.

It declares that each individual is only a carrier for the infinite ocean of knowledge and power that lies behind mankind. It teaches that wherever and whenever a desire, a want, or a prayer has been fulfilled, it has been done so from a supply of that infinite ocean and not from any supernatural being.

The *Raja Yogi* denies the existence of the supernatural, but stresses on two types of manifestations — the gross and the subtle. The subtle are the causes, while the gross, the effects; and while it is easy to perceive the gross, it is not so with the subtle. The practice of *Raja Yoga* helps in the perception of the subtle.

The *sutras* or aphorisms of Patanjali are the highest texts of *Raja Yoga* and it considers each soul as potentially divine, setting its own goal for manifesting this divinity within by controlling external and internal nature.

Knowledge is based on experience, and thus it is easy to find the truth propounded by the exact sciences. However, the same cannot be said of religion, which is based on faith and belief. But there is also an underlying universal belief — cutting across the different theories and the varying ideas of different sects in different countries — that is based upon universal experiences of the fountainheads of the different religions. These fountainheads, or original teachers, saw God, their inner soul and eternity and preached thus. It is possible to perceive that same experience through the practice of *Raja Yoga*.

The science of *Raja Yoga* puts forward a practical and scientifically worked out method to perceive this truth. *Raja Yoga* uses the instrument of mind both to 'see within', and to 'see beyond'. One needs to turn the mind inside, concentrate all its powers and direct the mind to analyse itself. It is a very difficult proposition, but is the only way to attain the knowledge of the eternity of the soul, which will then help remove all miseries and bring about perfect bliss.

Every human being has the right to ask the reason, or the 'why' of everything, and *Raja Yoga* teaches him to answer that question himself. A part of this practice is physical, but the main part is mental. The mind and the body are intricately connected, and the health of one depends on the health of the other. Thus, a healthy body is the abode of a healthy mind.

According to the *Raja Yogi*, the external world is the effect of one's own internal world, which is the actual cause. Thus, the person who learns to control the internal forces, can control the external ones too, and can thus be oblivious to 'nature's laws'. The progress and civilisation of the human race depends on controlling this nature.

This form of *Yoga* was discovered about 4,000 years ago; but while in India it fell into the hands of persons who destroyed ninety percent of the knowledge and tried to make great secret of the remainder, in the West it was shrouded in secrecy all through and regarded as mysticism, and people who wanted to practise it were either burned or killed after being branded witches and sorcerers. Mystery mongering weakens the human brain, and anything that is secret and mysterious should be rejected at once. Swamiji brought out *Raja Yoga* in public and while he explained those aphorisms that he could, the others he narrated from the books. He explained the *Sankhya* philosophy — upon which *Raja Yoga* is based — wherein external feelings are said to be received by the brain, which then relate it to the mind, wherefrom it is transmitted to the soul which perceives it. The mind is an instrument in the hands of the soul, and is constantly changing and vacillating. However, when perfected through *Yoga*, it can be trained to attach itself to any or all organs of the body. A glimpse of this power of concentration can be seen when in the simple urge to listen to a distant sound, the mind gets attached to the hearing organs only and the individual becomes oblivious to other sounds and concentrates only on the desired sound. This reflexive power is what the *Yogi* wants to attain, and the control of the instruments of the soul over the organs of the body is now also corroborated by modern physiologists. According to them, the senses, as observed by the various organs of the body, are transmitted to the brain, which then analyses through the mind and finally perceives the experience.

GYANA YOGA

Gyana Yoga is for rational people, and its *mantra* is '*Om Tat Sat*', implying that knowing *Om* is knowing the secret of the universe. The *Gyana Yogi* strives to realise God by the power of pure reason and through the true realisation of self.

The real 'I' is the eternal subject matter of knowledge, and could thus never be its object. It is beyond birth, death, fear, sense and thought. However, since knowledge cannot be had of the

Absolute but only of the related, man can thus theoretically realise himself as *Brahma* in this world itself. The *Vedas* constantly indicate the oneness of man with God, but few can penetrate the veil of *maya* and realise this truth.

The *Gyana Yogi* has to renounce fear and believe in nothing till he actually 'knows it'. He has to rid himself of his body, mind, and thought, and be content to know that he is only the *atman* or self. The Yogi, in search of this *atman*, or self, must fearlessly follow his reason to its farthest limits. The real 'I' is eternal and infinite, but layers of ignorance shields it from us. True *gyan* separates us completely from all matters and from all preconceived beliefs and lets us 'know' the *atman*.

The Sanskrit term *Vedanta* means the *anta*, or the conclusion of the *Vedas* — the earliest sacred literature of India — and it teaches us that *Brahma* alone is true and all else is *maya*, or illusion. This is also known as *Adwaitism*, or without dualism of good and evil, pleasure and pain, joy and sorrow; for *Brahma*, being perfect and the infinite Truth, is independent of all conditions of duality.

Although *Brahma* is one, yet in the relative plane, due to name and form, he appears to us as many. Just like earth is the real essence of the earthen jar, as it is of any other thing made of it, so is *Brahma* the true essence of all living beings. *Vedanta* goes ahead and proclaims that there is but one Being, and it manifests itself in full in every soul and not that the soul is only a part of that Being.

This truth about the soul is to be heard first. Once one has heard it, one must think about it; and once one has thought of it, one must meditate upon it by continuously telling oneself, 'I am He, I am He.' This is *Gyan Yoga*, the knowledge of God.

Swami Vivekananda continued his work in America till 1896. He spoke about Hinduism and was indeed the fiery champion of his Motherland. But to many Americans he was much more than this. While for some he opened the gates of wisdom, some found him possessing a 'kaleidoscopic genius', and some actually even proposed marriage to him.

During his very first year in America, Swamiji met many philosophers, scientists and artists, many of whom he was able to befriend, and some became his ardent devotees. His all-round personality influenced all who came in contact with him and it is said that the wealthy American financier John D. Rockfeller's first large donation to public welfare was the result of his meeting the Swami.

The lecture tour took its toll, and Swamiji, who was not accustomed to the severe winters of the Midwest, suffered intensely from cold. The extensive travelling — he was virtually moving every night from one city to an other on train — and then the intricate interactive discourses and lectures throughout the day, completely exhausted him by the end of the tour. The press was also constantly following his every lecture, and highlighted his patriotism, which showed up on many occasions. Then there were the occasional slander campaigns by the orthodox and narrow-minded Christian clergy, who felt slighted by his Parliament lectures. Swamiji handled these acts of small-minded fanaticism with sheer aloofness. He was in reverence of Christ and his teachings, but he was not afraid to be sternly critical of the destructive characteristics of present day Christianity, and would condemn the Christians' intolerance to such criticism, while they themselves kept on criticising, cursing and even abusing all heathens of the world.

The Slayton Bureau took advantage of the Swami's unworldly nature and started cheating him, whereupon some of his wellwishers got the contract annulled sometimes towards the end of February 1894. Thereafter Swamiji started lecturing independently again. But Swamiji was getting weary of this continuous lecturing. However, he resigned to the Divine will, and continued with his mission of spreading his message in the West. This time, however, he was centred at Chicago and toured the east coast, lecturing both at small private gatherings and before large public audiences. It was during this time that a certain Miss Mary Phillips of New York became his ardent follower.

The Swami was in Chicago till 28th June 1894, by which time even the Hindu society back home had not formally recognised him as its true representative. This jeopardised his entire mission, and his enemies in both the countries went on undeterred in their persistent campaign against him. The Christian missionaries were also disturbed with the sharp decrease in monetary contributions to their causes 'as a consequence of Vivekananda's success and teaching', and hence made a concerted effort to prove that his teachings were only personal and not of any Hindu sect or society, and were actually unacceptable to the Hindus themselves. The Brahmo Samaj and the Theosophical Society also felt slighted at the Swami's success in America and corroborated with the Christians in his persecution. Although initially Swamiji kept himself indifferent to such malicious attacks, gradually it grew into such menacing proportions that it became necessary to rein it, as otherwise the very purpose of his coming to America would have been defeated. He was therefore compelled to remind his countrymen of their duty; and on 9th April 1894, he wrote to Alasinga in Madras and advised him to take action in the form of convening a big meeting in Madras, which was to be presided over by some person of social standing, and wherein a resolution was to be adopted stating the satisfaction of the Hindus at Swamiji's representation of Hinduism in America. Subsequently, copies of this were to be sent to the leading newspapers of America. Although the King of Khetri and the *Dewan* of Junagadh wrote to Swamiji, and even to Mr. Hale, supporting his cause, yet they did not dent as much, and the press this time had set their guns on Swamiji and restricted their printing to the anti-Swami movement in India.

But while the Indian people were indeed slow to respond to Swamiji's success at the Parliament of Religions and in thanking the American people for extending such a hearty welcome to him in America, they were actually not slow in responding to his call. Actually, even before Swamiji's letter reached Alasinga, the people of Madras had already arranged a public meeting in his honour on 28th April. Another such meeting was also held in Calcutta under the auspices of Dharampala, the Secretary of the Maha Bodhi Society, Ceylon and also a co-attendee at the Chicago Parliament as the representative of the Society. Large meetings were held in other cities as well and soon Swami Vivekananda became a household name in India.

A letter intimating Swamiji of the Buddhist monk Dharampala's meeting in Calcutta reached him on or about 9th July 1894 and was the first news of India's public action in this regard. It relieved him immensely. Soon after, Swamiji also received Alasinga's earlier letter from Madras intimating him of the 28th April meeting there. But it was only towards the end of August 1894, that the news of the Madras Meeting was published in some of America's leading newspapers, and this cleared the air of all doubts about Swami Vivekananda representing the Hindus of India. News of the other meetings also thus started pouring in.

Towards the end of July, Swamiji was invited by Sarah Farmer to the Greenacres Conferences, which was open to all religious speakers who had something to say, and to all men and women with a desire to learn. Here, he held a series of classes — his first in the West but predictive of the shape that his American work was to take up later — that expounded the *Vedanta* philosophy to a group of enthusiastic students who sat around him under a pine tree. He taught them the *Gita* and *Raja Yoga* too. The Swami was at Greenacres for about two weeks, after which he went to Plymouth where he was invited to speak before the Free Religious Association. From Plymouth, Swamiji travelled to

the seaside village of Annisquam in Massachusetts, and thereby completed a full circle by returning to the same place where exactly a year ago he had been the guest of Dr. J.H.Wright who had given him the letters of introduction for the Parliament of Religions. This time of course he was the guest of his ever-loyal friend, Mrs. Bagley of Detroit, and remained there for two weeks.

The summer being over, Swamiji left Annisquam on 6th September for Boston. There he had three-weeks of lecture engagements. From here, he went to Cambridge, where he stayed at the house of Mrs. Bull, the widow of a famous Norwegian violinist and later on one of Swamiji's most ardent supporters. His next stop was Baltimore, Maryland where he spoke twice — on 14th and 21st October on 'Dynamic Religion'. From Baltimore, the Swami went to Washington, from where he once again returned to Baltimore in the first week of November.

By this time, Swamiji had made up his mind to remain in the West for some more time. But he now wished to gain some earnest and sincere disciples to whom he could teach the *Adwaita Vedanta* and who could then disseminate the same. To this end, in November 1894, he organised a Vedanta Society in New York, where he was to settle down soon in early 1895 after he finished his present engagements — as scheduled by Mrs. Bull — at Cambridge and at Brooklyn. At Cambridge, Swamiji also gave a stirring lecture on *The Ideals of Indian Women*, which moved the women of Cambridge so much that, unknown to Swamiji, on the occasion of Christmas that year, they sent a touching letter, along with a beautiful picture of Jesus and Mary, to 'The Mother of Swami Vivekananda' in far away India. On 28th December

Swami Vivekananda at Greenacres.

Swamiji left for Brooklyn to speak at the Ethical Association there, whose President was Dr. Lewis G. Janes, an earlier acquaintance of Swamiji.

Although Swamiji did set up a permanent address in New York — somewhere towards the end of January 1895 — at 54 West 33rd Street — from where he started giving regular free lectures specially on *Raja Yoga* and *Gyana Yoga* — it was only in June that he could finally put to practice his dream of an intensive training course for a small group of selected disciples. By this time he had a number of disciples: Madam Marie Louise and Leon Landsberg, who were his first proclaimed American disciples and who were later initiated and given the names of Swamis Abhayananda and Kripananda respectively. There were also others like Ole Bull, Dr. Allan Day, Ellen Waldo, Mary Phillips, Prof. Wyman, Prof. Wright, Dr. Street, Francis Leggett, Josephine McLeod, and a widow named Mrs. Sturgis. This course was held at the retreat of Miss Dutcher, another student, at the Thousand Island Park in New York. He began this course around 19th June and spoke to the small group, day and night, on various topics, including the Bible, *bhakti*, *nishtha* or persistence, balance between *tamas*, *rajas* and *sattva*, i.e. idleness, activity and self-illumination, the *Gita*, the Upanishads, Buddha and *nirvana*, or final emancipation of the soul, the different Hindu sects, *Vedanta*, the Yogas, and of course Sri Ramakrishna and Mother Kali. It continued till 6th August, and Miss Ellen Waldo, Mrs.Funke, Miss Christine Greenstidel, Dr.Wright and Miss Ruth Ellis are some of the best known attendees to these sessions. Their notes were later on compiled as 'Inspired Talks', which has some of the most dramatic utterances on these topics. It was during this time that he also composed the poem, 'Song of the Sanyasi'. Meanwhile, he received pressing invitations from England, and Swamiji decided to travel first to Paris with Mrs. Leggett or the earlier Mrs. Sturgis and then to England.

At London, Swamiji was received by Mr. Sturdy and Miss Henrietta Müller, and was initially the guest of the latter at her house in Cambridge, from where he moved to Sturdy's place at Reading. Sturdy was already a *Vedantist* and mastered his knowledge of Sanskrit from Swamiji, who helped him to translate the *Narada-Bhakti-Sutras* into English during his six-week stay with him. Swamiji spent the months of September and October visiting the places of historic and artistic interests in England.

The English people received Swamiji quite warmly, and he was happy to find that the 'Negro' phobia of America was totally absent in England. His first lecture in England, on 'Self-Knowledge', was delivered on the 22nd October at Prince's Hall in Piccadilly. It was well received by the audience and acclaimed by the British press. He next spoke at the Chelsea residence of Rev. H.R. Haweis, who had heard him earlier at the Parliament of Religions.

Towards the end of the month, Swamiji found lodgings at 80 Oakley Street at Chelsea, where he took regular classes, which were almost always overcrowded and people had to sit on the floor. During this period he also lectured at clubs, societies and even private drawing rooms carrying out his mission of spreading Sri Ramakrishna's teachings as far and wide as he could. As in New York, so in England, Swamiji worked very hard and without respite, teaching all that he knew to all those who came to him. His circle of influence was also increasing steadily, and he found many people coming forward to help him propagate the teachings of *Vedanta*.

Lady Isabel Margesson was one of the first to call on Swamiji at his Oakley Street residence. She was very impressed with Swamiji's teachings, and on one Sunday in November that year, invited him to speak at her residence at 63 St. George's Road. One of the attendees was a lady highly interested in educational work, Margaret Nobel. She was the

Swami Vivekananda in London, December 1896.

principal of a school that she owned and an outstanding member of the Sesame Club, of which lady Margesson was the Secretary. Miss Nobel carefully weighed the Swami's words, but found it difficult to accept them at face value. It took several months to accept Swamiji's philosophy, and it was only when he was leaving England towards the end of November, that she addressed him as 'Master'. She became one of the most devoted disciples of Swamiji, but, in true spirit of her Master's teaching, she accepted his sayings only after she was convinced of their contents.

In all his speeches and talks in England, Swamiji invariably spoke about the important tenets of Hinduism, especially about *Vedanta* philosophy, and answered the many questions that he was besieged with. His first hand experience of the English society revolutionised his ideas about the English people, and even during this short sojourn of about three months only, he was able to lay down an unshakable foundation on which he could build anytime in the future.

Swamiji soon started receiving letters from America asking him to return to continue with his work there, the opportunity for which was just ripe then. On the other hand, his English disciples wanted him to settle down in England and continue working there. Swamiji had envisaged such a situation and had written to the Belur *Math* as far back as in September itself to send a competent monk for the work in England, and had even forwarded the passage money. Accordingly, he was expecting Swami Saradananda to arrive before his departure for America. However, Swami Saradananda was yet to arrive when Swamiji left England on 27th November 1895, once more for America.

J.J. Goodwin.

Swamiji was back in New York on 6th December 1895, and was happy to find that Madam Marie Louise, Leon Landsberg and Sarah Ellen Waldo had kept the embers burning in his absence. In order to keep together the introductory work initiated earlier, Swamiji resumed classes for the reading and study of the *Bhagvad Gita*, and other allied subjects. He moved into a more spacious headquarters at 228 West 39th Street, from where he started regular scriptural classes and taught the four *Yogas*. His disciples now made arrangements to record the extempore lectures of Swamiji for posterity, and it was mainly due to the tireless efforts of Swamiji's 'faithful Goodwin' — who accompanied Swamiji wherever he went — that much of his thoughts and teachings could be preserved.

This time Swamiji was more organised, and although he did give public lectures, he carried on regularly with the classes at the 39th Street address, the attendance at both increasing day by day. He continued to preach about God, Love, and Truth, but the moves of his critics, and those who wanted to use him for their own ends, often disturbed his peace. The Free-thinkers, comprising of atheists, materialists, agnostics and rationalists, invited Swamiji to speak at their society, and although the invitation was extended to show their followers how easily religious claims could be refuted by the powerful arguments of logic and science, it was Swami Vivekananda who, being as familiar with logic and science as with *Adwaita* philosophy, ruled the roost and proved himself a master in wielding their own weapons. The powerful effect of the lecture had many a member of the society come to him the next day and sit at his feet to listen to his religious sermons. Thus, Swamiji had a large and ever-increasing following among both men and women drawn from the most heterogeneous classes of society, coming to him with the sincere desire to pursue truth for truth's sake.

The records of Swamiji's speeches and the various write-ups were published regularly in the Indian magazine *Brahmavadin*, which was launched by his disciples in Madras in September 1895 with his active support and financing. His fame as an orator spread with lightning speed in New York, and soon the 1,500 seat capacity Madison Square Garden had to be hired for his second series of Sunday lectures which he gave in February 1896. Swamiji was soon reckoned as a spiritual guide and teacher 'whose sublime philosophy is slowly and surely permeating the ethical atmosphere of our country (America).' His *Adwaita Vedanta* knew no bounds of creeds and dogmas, and was 'uplifting, purifying, infinitely comforting, and … based on the love of God', and thus attracted the intelligentsia of America and sowed the seeds of a spiritual awakening there. People thronged the libraries to read whatever they could on India and Hindu philosophy, and were quick to appreciate the religious philosophy that appeals to the heart and reason alike, and 'satisfies all the religious cravings of human nature'. Among the notable devotees that Swamiji acquired this time were the French actress Sarah Bernhardt, the pastor of a fashionable Plymouth Congregational Church Dr. Lyman Abbott, and the electrical scientist Nicola Tesla, who thought that he could prove mathematically Swamiji's rendition of the rational theories of the *kalpas* (time cycles), *prana* (life) and *akash* (ether), as described in the *Sankhya* philosophy and which could be applied by modern science to solve many a cosmological problem. By February 1896 Swamiji had initiated three Americans — Madam Marie Louise, Leon Landsberg and Dr. Street, all very worldly people with learning, position, and culture — as *sanyasis*, and several young men and women as *brahmacharis*.

Swami Vivekananda had founded the *Vedanta Society* in New York quite some time back, and he now wanted his American disciples and devotees to take active part in spreading the teachings of Sri Ramakrishna to the English-speaking world. Thus he conferred Sarah Ellen Waldo, who became Sister Haridasi, with spiritual powers and authority to preach the *Vedanta*. He also started training the other *sanyasis* and some selected devotees towards the same end, so that they could continue and further the cause of the *Vedanta* in America when he left.

Swami Vivekananda discovered that the *Vedanta* philosophy, across its three stages of *Dwaita*, *Visishtha-Dwaita*, and *A-Dwaita*, encompassed the philosophy of all religions. Whereas *Vedanta*, applied to the various ethnic customs and creeds of India, explains Hinduism; the *Dwaita* stage, when applied to the ethnic groups of Europe, expounds Christianity, and when applied to the Semitic groups, defines Mohammedanism; and the *Yoga* perception form of the *A-Dwaita* stage elucidates Buddhism. The different applications of *Vedanta* vary according to different needs, surroundings and other circumstances of not only different ethnic groups, but also different creeds and cults. Thus, we have different sects like *Shaivas*, *Shaktas*, *Vaishnavites*, etc…. Swamiji took it upon himself 'to put the Hindu ideas into English and then make out of dry philosophy and intricate mythology and queer startling psychology, a religion which shall be easy, simple, popular, and at the same time meet the requirements of the highest minds.' Always stressing on the universal and humanistic side of the *Vedas*, Vivekananda infused vigour into Hindu thought and thus, overshadowing the prevalent pacifism, he presented this Hindu spirituality to the West.

According to Swamiji, 'A *sanyasi* cannot belong to any religion, for his is a life of independent thought, which draws from all religions; his is a life of realization, not merely of

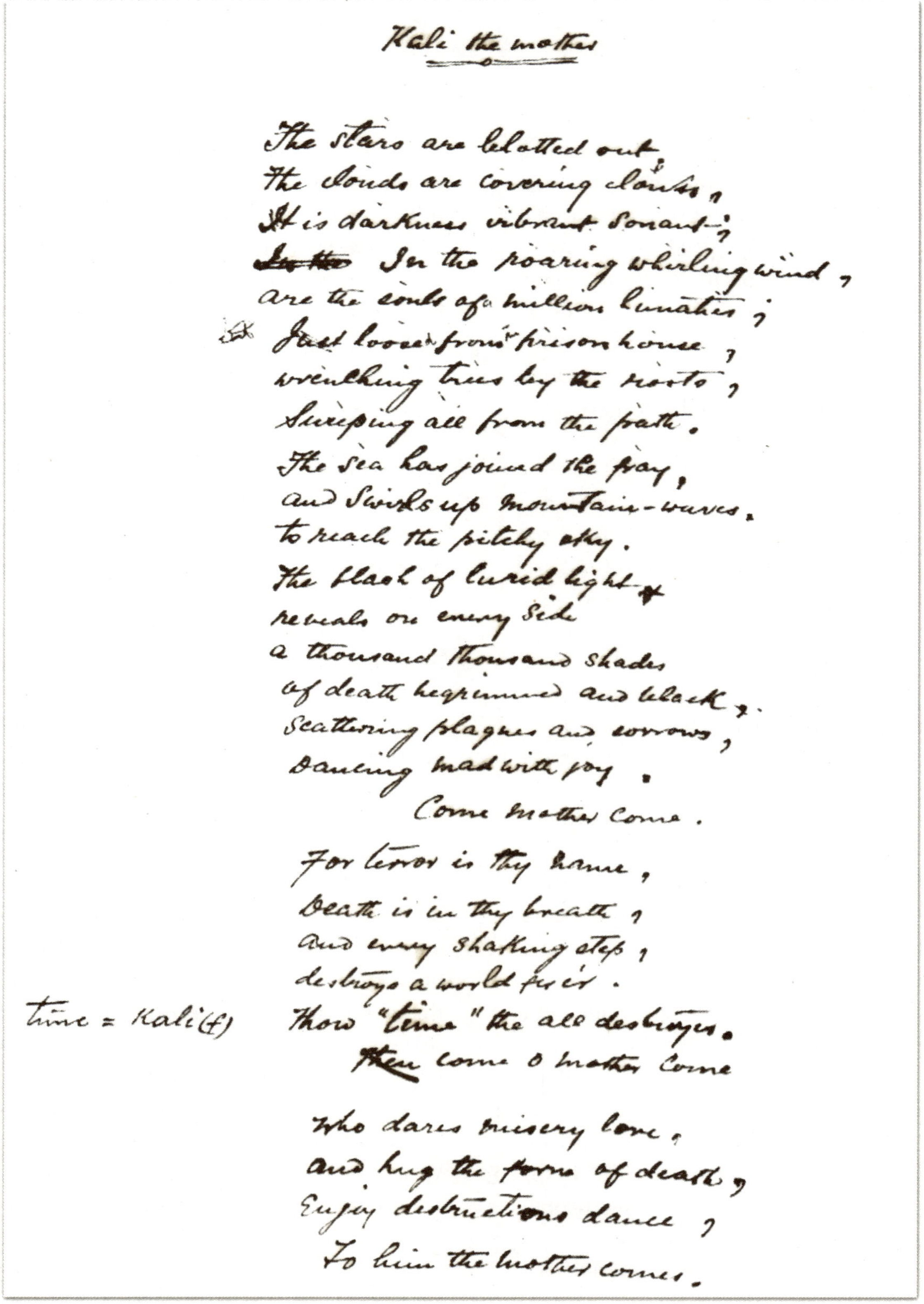

Kali the mother

The stars are blotted out,
The clouds are covering clouds,
It is darkness vibrant sonant,
~~In the~~ In the roaring whirling wind,
Are the souls of a million lunatics;
Just loosed from prison house,
wrenching trees by the roots,
Sweeping all from the path.
The sea has joined the fray,
And swirls up mountain-waves.
to reach the pitchy sky.
The flash of lurid light
reveals on every side
a thousand thousand shades
of death begrimmed and black,
Scattering plagues and sorrows,
Dancing mad with joy.
        Come mother come.

For terror is thy name,
Death is in thy breath,
And every shaking step,
destroys a world for ever.
Thou "time" the all destroyer.
        then come O mother come

who dares misery love,
and hug the form of death,
Enjoy destruction's dance,
To him the mother comes.

time = Kali (f)

Facsimile of Swami Vivekananda's handwriting.

theory or belief, much less of dogma', and *Vedanta* is the sum total of the *darshana*, or philosophical outlook of the *rishis*, or sages, contributing to the Vedas through the ages. Swamiji's contribution to *Vedanta* could be summed up as comprising the nine salient points of: Truth is God and that religion is in everything; 'That God, for whom you have been searching all over the universe is all the time yourself — your self, not in the personal sense but in the Impersonal...'; 'Without the *Vedanta* every religion is superstition; with it everything becomes religion.' *Adwaita* accepts dualism and all systems preceding it, and is the universal solvent into which all philosophies merge at last; Religion must be presented rationally, and its study should be pursued scientifically; All truths should be made available to all people — '*Adwaita* shall no more be a secret ... it must come down to the everyday life of the people;' Everyone should embody all phases of truth — the need of today is the allrounder, one in whom all the elements of philosophy, mysticism, emotion and work were equally present in full; All paths are to be made active in the service of Man as God — 'Feel that the receiver is the higher one. You serve the other because you are lower than he, not because he is low and you are high;' Religion must busy itself with the making of the man — building of character is more important than penances and meditations; and 'Worship of the Terrible' — do not fear even death, and worship Mother Kali, whose hands hold good and bad, sweetness and terror.

After spending about four months in America, wduring which he toured Detroit, Boston, Chicago and other places, and spoke at various forums, including the Graduate Philosophical Club of the Harvard University, and

Professor Max Müller.

progressed in creating an establishment in America which could take care of itself, Swamiji again sailed for England on 15th April 1896 on the *S.S. Germanic* for another season of strenuous teaching there. In less than three years of work in America, he had made a profound and indelible impression among its people, and was able to remove the deep-rooted bigotry that had existed there towards India and Hinduism.

Landing at Liverpool, he left for Reading where he was once again the guest of Edward Sturdy. Swami Saradananda preceded him in England, and was at Reading to receive him. He had brought all the news from India, and Vivekananda was immensely happy to see a brother-disciple after so many years. Sturdy had rented a house at 63 St. George's Road in Southwest London to facilitate Swamiji's work, and soon Vivekananda shifted there with Swami Saradananda, his constant companion cum secretary and personal attendant Goodwin, his American acquaintance John P. Fox, and his own younger brother Mahendranath Dutta, who was in London for higher education. Swamiji began to hold regular classes there from the first week of May itself, and these continued till the middle of July 1896. He also gave several invitation lectures at various clubs and at the residences of his admirers.

One of the memorable events of Swami Vivekananda's second visit to England was his meeting the celebrated Orientalist professor Max Müller at his Oxford residence on 28th May 1896, shortly after the Professor had completed an article on Sri Ramakrishna, entitled 'A Real Mahatma'. Prof. Müller was eager to know more about the Master, and asked, 'What are you doing to make him known to the world?' He assured

Swamiji that he would write a larger and fuller account of the Master's life and teachings provided he received more facts and details. Swamiji at once instructed Swami Saradananda to write to the India and get as many details as possible on the Master. The result was Prof. Müller's latter work *Ramakrishna: His Life and Sayings*.

Vivekananda found that the growing work in both the continents required resident *sanyasis* from home. He thus sent Swami Saradananda to America and summoned Swami Abhedananda to England. He was then thirty-three years old, a mature man, full of love for people of all walks of life. By the middle of 1896, Sturdy's translation of the *Narada-Sutras on Bhakti-Yoga*, to which Swamiji had written commentaries, had become quite popular. Swamiji's own works on *Karma-Yoga, Raja-Yoga* and *Patanjali's Yoga Aphorisms* had been published in America, and his treatise on *Bhakti-Yoga* was to be published from Madras in September that year.

Swamiji worked harder during his second visit to England, and was happy with the work here, which was 'much better and deeper than in the U.S.' Swamiji's central motive was 'to preach unto mankind their divinity, and how to make it manifest in every moment of life'. He found ignorance to be at the root of all miseries, and called upon 'the earth's bravest and the best' to 'sacrifice themselves for the good of many, for the welfare of all'. His call captivated many distinguished intellectuals of the British society, and he gathered some of the most diligent and heroic workers and helpers in his cause during this visit. His earlier acquaintances like Sturdy, Henrietta Müller and Margaret Nobel now became his disciples, ready to sacrifice everything for him and his cause, as did some new associates like Captain Henry Sevier and his wife Charlotte Sevier.

In London, July marked the end of the lecture season and the beginning of the holiday season. Thus, Swamiji accepted the invitation of the Seviers and Miss Müller to accompany them for a tour and holiday of the European continent. Swamiji was elated with the prospect of visiting Switzerland and the Alps. During that tour, the entourage visited Calais, Paris, Geneva, Chamonix and the Alps. The Alps fascinated Swamiji beyond words and he expressed his desire to set up a monastery in similar surroundings somewhere. This desire was later realized by the Seviers after three years at Mayavati in the Indian Himalayas. In the Alps, Swamiji and his companions visited Little St. Bernard, Zermatt, and finally rested for two weeks at Saas-Fee in the Upper Rhone valley of Switzerland. At the invitation of the German Orientalist Paul Deussen — who had recently returned from India and was also deeply interested in the *Vedanta* philosophy — they left Saas-Fee and proceeded, via Lucerne, Schaffhausen, Heidelberg, Coblenz, Cologne and Berlin, to Kiel in Germany. The natural beauty of the Alps awed Swamiji. He also visited every monument and place of historical importance at each of these places. Prof. Deussen was eloquent of his visit to India, its culture, and its hospitality, but was appalled at the existing poverty. He joined the Swami's entourage and maintained the group count back to England by filling in the place emptied by Miss Müller who had travelled back to England from Switzerland itself.

The six-week holiday did much good to the worn-out health of Vivekananda, and he was now eager to return to London to work again with renewed vigour. Accordingly, the group returned to England via Hamburg, Amsterdam and Harwich, and reached London on 17th September 1896.

After staying for a few days at the Seviers' place in Hampstead, Swamiji commenced his work afresh in London from Airlie Lodge, the Ridgeway Gardens residence of Miss Müller. His weekday classes resumed from 39 Victoria Street, London from 8th October onwards. In the meantime, Swami Abhedanand had arrived from India, and Swamiji impressed upon him the responsibilities of his new life. Swamiji was so happy with the progress of his

Swami Vivekananda,
London, December 1896.

work in England that he wrote back to his Indian disciples that with just twenty earnest minded and capable preachers of *Vedanta*, he could revolutionise the West in as many years. Both Prof. Deussen and Prof. Max Müller were in constant communication with him, and assured him of their complete support for his movement.

Apart from the regular lectures at the Victoria Street address, Swamiji also spoke at clubs and other social gatherings on invitation, which included churches both in London and Oxford. Swamiji's speeches endeared him to many, including the authors Frederick Myers and Edward Carpenter, and other intelligentsia like Moncure Conway, Dr. Stanton Coit, Rev. Charles Voysey, Canon Hugh Haweis, and Canon Basil Wilberforce.

Although busy with his weekly classes and in lectures and interviews, he was constantly thinking about his work in India, and of establishing a women's *Math* there. He now contemplated on going back to India in the coming winter. Back home, the *Brahmavadin* was constantly disseminating Swamiji's teachings and ideas, and since July 1896, an English language monthly, the *Prabudha Bharat,* was also being published from Madras. Swamiji was also delighted at the success of the maiden speech delivered in England by Swami Abhedananda. Swamiji was also glad to know of Swami Saradananda's success and growing influence in America, and the progress of the *Vedanta* work there with the active participation of Sarah Ellen Waldo and Mrs. Bull. Amongst the Indian dignitaries who witnessed Swamiji's establishing 'a golden relation between England and India' from close quarters was Sri Bepin Chandra Pal, of the later Lal-Bal-Pal fame.

Since October 1896 itself, Vivekananda began to write to all his wellwishers about his confirmed plans to return to India and commence his work there on a small scale. The Indian famine of November 1896 convinced Swamiji of his calling there. His London disciples donated generously towards the cause, and he sent the subscriptions to India for relief work to be undertaken by the Ramakrishna Order, the stress being on social service even through religious activities. It was sometime in the second week of November that, at the instance of Swamiji, the Seviers bought four tickets to India — one for Swamiji, one for Goodwin and the remaining two for themselves. Swamiji at once wrote to his disciples in Madras that he would leave for India in the last week of December. He also expressed his desire to establish two centres in India, one in Calcutta and the other in Madras, and informed them of the Seviers's desire to found a Himalayan centre. 'We will begin with these three centres, and later on we will get to Bombay and Allahabad. And from these points, if the Lord is pleased, we will invade not only India, but send bands of preachers to every country in the world.'

Swamiji's last lecture in England was on *Adwaita Vedanta* on 10th December. His English students gave him a grand farewell reception on 13th December at the Royal Society of Painters in Piccadilly, where Sturdy gave a very touching speech. On the 16th, Swamiji and the Seviers left London for Italy, where they intended to visit some of its important cities before boarding their ship, the *Prinz Regent Luitpoid,* which was to leave Naples on the 30th. While Goodwin joined them directly at Naples, Swamiji and the Seviers visited Milan, Pisa, Florence and Rome en route Naples, and extensively toured the cathedrals, museums and art galleries at each of these places. They attended the High Mass at St. Peter's on Christmas, the pageantry and ostentations of which repulsed him and prompted him to say, 'Can it be possible that the Church that practices that display, pomp and gorgeous ceremonial is really the follower of the lowly Jesus who had nowhere to lay His head?'

On his way back to India, Swamiji visited Aden, and finally, on 15th January 1897 *S.S. Prinz Regent Luitpod* docked in at Colombo, then under the same British rule as India.

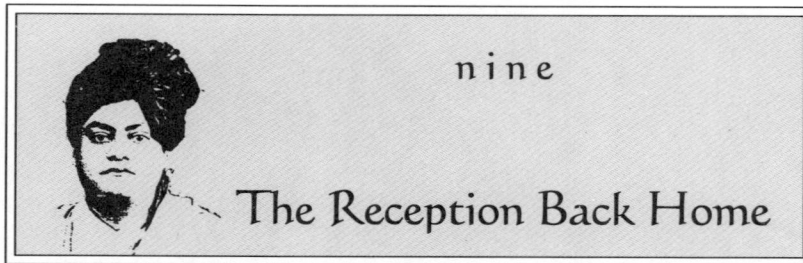

The news of Swami Vivekananda's return had preceded him. This time India was ready to make up for its earlier folly of according recognition so late to one of its foremost sons who had virtually conquered the two western continents with his *Vedanta* movement. His brother-disciple Swami Nirajananda was already there in Colombo to receive him. In addition, there were representatives of various religious sects and social bodies who had come to welcome him home, and his fellow-countrymen had formed reception committees in almost all the cities across the nation. Newspapers and journals across the country came out with series of editorials praising him and his work.

As *S.S. Prinz Regent Luitpod* docked into Colombo on the evening of 15th January 1897, the shouts and clappings of the sea of people drowned the noise of the breaking waves of the Indian Ocean. A horse driven carriage took Swamiji to Barnes Street where a canopy had been erected to give him a public welcome. Another canopy had been erected in front of the bungalow on Cinnamon Gardens where arrangements were made for his temporary stay, and Swamiji was taken there in a procession from the first. The honours were done by P. Coomaraswamy, a member of the Legislative Council. Swamiji responded by pointing out that 'the spirituality of the Hindus is revealed by the princely reception which they have given to a begging *sanyasi*.'

Swamiji's first public lecture in the East was delivered at the Floral Hall on the evening of 16th January, where he spoke on *India, the Holy Land.* Thereafter, all throughout his four days' stay at Colombo, he gave several lectures and met people from all walks of life who thronged to him. He had originally planned to take a steamer straight from Colombo to Madras; but several telegrams from various towns of Ceylon and South India reached him at Colombo begging him to visit their respective towns so he had to alter his plans and proceed overland.

On the morning of 19th January, Swamiji left Colombo by train for Kandy, and after a day's stay there, the party left by coach for Jaffna en route Anuradhapuram located at the northern tip of Ceylon. Swamiji was welcomed enthusiastically everywhere. At Anuradhapuram, the Swami spoke under a 2000-year-old sacred *Bodhi* tree to a motley crowd of some 3,000 strong. However, Swamiji

Swamiji in Colombo, January 1897.

could not complete his address as a large crowd of some fanatical *bhikkus* and their followers obstructed him, and Swamiji had to restrain the Hindus to avoid a serious clash. A group of leading Hindu citizens of Jaffna was waiting to receive him at the Elephant Pass, situated some twelve miles ahead of the town of Jaffna. Here a bridge connected the island of Jaffna to the main island of Ceylon, and Swamiji was taken from here — in a procession of some 10,000 people — to the town where virtually every house was decorated in his honour. A grand welcome awaited him at the Hindu College at Jaffna on the evening of that Sunday, 24th January 1897, and afterwards a 15,000 strong torch procession was taken out. In this last leg of his travel through what is today known as Sri Lanka, Swamiji was at Jaffna for two days, after which, he left for Rameswaram by boat on 26th January.

The Raja of Ramnad, Bhaskara Sethupathi, came to Pamban Roads in his state boat to receive Swamiji personally, and the people of Pamban gave him a tremendous ovation. He was seated in the state carriage, which was pulled through the town not by the horses but by the Raja and the people. Swamiji was there at Pamban for three days during which he visited the Rameswaram temple, which had seen the culmination of his pilgrimage through India prior to his leaving for America. The Raja erected a forty feet high monument, with the inscriptions *Satyameva Jayate* at the spot where Swamiji had first set his foot on the Indian soil after his triumph in the West.

Swamiji left Ramnad around midnight of 31st January and travelled northwards to Madurai via Paramakkudi and Manamadurai. Everywhere he was given rousing welcomes and he spoke about various aspects of Indian spirituality and western materialism and how the two supplemented and complemented each other. Swamiji arrived at Madurai on 2nd February and visited the Meenakshi temple the day after.

From Madurai, he took the train to Kumbakonam. At every station en route to Kumbakonam, thousands of people greeted him. He stayed at Kumbakonam for three days. The same enthusiastic welcome awaited Swamiji at the railway stations en route his journey to Madras from Kumbakonam. His popularity amongst the general masses was brought out at a small railway station away from Madras where the people forced Swamiji's train to stop by lying down on the railway tracks. Visibly moved by this expression of love, the Swami came out of his carriage and appeared before the people, thanking them and blessing them.

Madras was brimming for weeks with enthusiasm for the homecoming of Swami Vivekananda, and a Vivekananda Reception Committee — comprising the intelligentsia of the city and the disciples of Swami Vivekananda — was formed under the leadership of Justice Subrahmanya Iyer. Leaflets bearing Swamiji's achievements in the West were distributed, subscriptions were collected, and large scale preparations were made to receive him on his arrival at Madras. The railway station and the streets were lavishly decorated, and arches were erected throughout the route from Egmore railway station to Castle Kernan-the earlier Ice House which is now known as the Vivekananda House - via Chintradipet, Napier Road, Mount Road, Pycroft's Road and Beach Road. It was Madras that had first recognised Vivekananda's inherent powers and contributed towards his journey to the Parliament of Religions, and was thus now proud to welcome back 'the undoubtedly great man who has done so much to raise the prestige of his motherland' to the world.

Thunderous applause greeted the train carrying the Swami as it entered Egmore station at around 7.30 on the morning of 6th February. Hundreds of people of all ages thronged the railway station, entrance to which had to be regulated due to the constraint of space within, and welcomed Swamiji with deafening cheers and clapping of hands. Swamiji drove to Castle Kernan in a carriage that moved very slowly and halted repeatedly to enable the multitudes to make offerings to their beloved and venerated Swami. The ladies performed *aarti*, or the traditional waving of lamps in worship before him; the people garlanded him; and the students un-harnessed the horses and pulled the carriage themselves with great enthusiasm. Never in the history of Madras was such an enthusiastic reception accorded to anyone, either European or Indian. In the days to come, Swamiji attended several welcome programmes and addressed the gatherings on building a national spiritual life in India on modern lines.

In the nine days that he stayed at Madras, he was besieged by visitors of all classes and of both sexes. There were crowds constantly waiting before the Castle at all hours of the day and night. The Raja of Khetri sent his private secretary, Munshi Jagmohanlal, all the way to Madras to convey his personal welcome address to Swamiji. The local people took him as an *avatar*, or incarnation, of the *Shaiva* saint Sambandha Swami and worshipped him. Over 10,000 people assembled in and around the Victoria Hall where Swamiji was given the main welcome address on 7th February. To control the crowds, entry to all his meetings had to be regulated by tickets, the proceeds of which was to be devoted to further his work in India. He was constantly meeting people and lecturing throughout his stay in Madras.

The difference between the unknown wanderer of 1892, and the famous Swami of 1897 is best borne out in the writings of Prof. Sundararama Iyer's son, K. S. Ramaswami Sastri, who had met Swamiji on both occasions. He wrote, 'In 1892 he looked like one who had a tryst with destiny and was not quite sure when or where or

how he was to keep that tryst. But in 1897 he looked like one who had kept the tryst with destiny, who clearly knew his mission, and who was confident about its fulfilment. He walked with steady and unfaltering steps and went along his predestined path, issuing commands and being sure of loyal obedience.'

Swamiji's last public lecture in Madras was on the evening of 14th February in front of 3,000 listeners at the Harmston Circus Pavilion where he spoke on *The Future of India*. He opened his lecture by reiterating India's past glory and urged his audience to 'build an India yet greater than what she was' by studying the gems of spirituality that are stored in the religious books and sharing them with everyone by teaching these in languages understood by the masses. He continued, 'For the next fifty years this alone shall be our keynote — this, our great Mother India.... The first of all worship is the worship of the *Virat* — of those all around us … and the first gods we have to worship are our countrymen.' He concluded by saying that, 'We must have a hold on the spiritual and secular education of the nation.... We must have life-building, man-making, character-making assimilation of ideas.'

Swamiji would say that 'India will awake again if anyone could love with all his heart the people of the country — bereft of the grace of affluence, of blasted fortune, their discretion totally lost, down-trodden, ever-starved, quarrelsome, and envious. Then only will India awake, when hundreds of large hearted men and women, giving up all desires of enjoying the luxuries of life, will long and exert themselves to their utmost for the well-being of the millions of their countrymen who are gradually sinking lower and lower in the vortex of destitution and ignorance.'

The Swami received constant invitations to visit the other cities of India. But he was tired and worn out by hard work and the heat in Madras. So, on Monday, the 15th of February, Swamiji boarded the *S.S. Mombasa* to sail straight to Calcutta. He was given a warm farewell by a distinguished gathering as well as the common people of Madras at the harbour pier.

The whole of Bengal, and Calcutta in particular, was eagerly following Swamiji's victorious march since his return from the West, and readying itself to give the triumphant son of the soil a befitting welcome. A meeting was called at the residence of Raja Benoy Krishna Deb Bahadur to form a Reception Committee for the occasion. The Maharaja of Darbhanga became the President of this committee and *Babu* Narendranath Sen, editor of the *Indian Mirror*, was appointed Honorary Secretary. The Reception Committee made elaborate preparations to receive Swamiji. The entire route from the Sealdah railway station — where he would disembark from the train after boarding it from Budge-Budge on getting off the steamer — to Ripon College, where he was to be formally received by the citizenry, was colourfully festooned and arches were set up at all the street crossings. Two people were also despatched to Budge-Budge to receive Swamiji there and to inform him of their plans.

(opp.): Swamiji in Madras, February 1897.

The Swami was also expectantly looking forward to his return to the city of his birth. As the steamer sailed up the Hooghly, Swamiji pointed out all the places of interest on both sides of the river to the Seviers and the other disciples accompanying him. *S.S. Mombasa* anchored at Budge-Budge on the night of 18th February, and Swamiji, accompanied by Swami Shivananda, Swami Niranjanananda, the Seviers, Goodwin, and some of his disciples from Madras, including the editors of *Brahmavadin* and *Prabudha Bharat*, boarded a special train for Sealdah early next morning, that is Friday, the 19th of February.

The special train arrived at Sealdah station precisely at 7:30 am, and the station area was besieged by a 20,000 strong crowd of people from the entire cross section of the society. As soon as Swamiji alighted from the train, the members of the Reception Committee stepped forward and took him to a bedecked phaeton commissioned for the occasion. The Swami and the members of his party were garlanded and heartily applauded as the phaeton inched its way amidst the cheering multitude. People also crowded the verandas and rooftops of the houses along the road, and a stream of carriages followed the Swami's. En route, some young men in the welcoming crowd unyoked the horses of the Swami's carriage and drew it themselves right up to Ripon College.

At the Ripon College on Harrington Street — which is now known as the Mahatma Gandhi Road — the Honourable Charu Chunder Mitter escorted Swamiji to the dais, where he modestly bowed to the crowd and gave a very short speech of thanks for welcoming him in such a grand manner. Thereafter, Swamiji and his party left for Babu Pashupatinath Bose's house at Baghbazar, from where Swamiji proceeded to the *Math* at Alambazar. Meanwhile accommodation for his entourage was made at the riverside mansion of Gopal Lal Seal at Cossipore.

At Alambazar, Vivekananda's brother-disciples had made their own arrangements to receive their leader. Whereas all the other brother-disciples present there had gone to Sealdah to receive Swamiji, Swami Akhandananda and Swami

Reception for Swamiji in Calcutta on February 28, 1897.

In Calcutta, February 1897.

Ramakrishnananda remained at the *Math* to make arrangements for the ceremonial reception of Swamiji. The monks at the Alambazar *Math* were elated to have their beloved Naren back amongst them. On his arrival at the *Math*, Swamiji was welcomed by the two Swamis, and then taken inside. Swamiji spent the nights at the *Math*, and the days at Seal's mansion, meeting and speaking to the incessant flow of people who came to pay their respects and hear him speak on *Vedanta*. With his brother monks he shared the nostalgia of their days with their Master and told them of his experiences of his wandering days and of the West.

The welcome address was scheduled to be delivered at 4 pm on Sunday, 28th February at Raja Sir Radhakanta Deb Bahadur's palace at Shovabazar. It was announced that free tickets would be issued in order to control the number of entrees, and these tickets were to be collected prior to the function. In spite of this, the place was crowded to its utmost capacity, with some 4,000 people covering every available inch on the spacious quadrangle and the verandas surrounding it. The native elite of the capital of the erstwhile British Empire in India was present at one of the most distinguished gatherings ever in the city to welcome a 'Prince among men, a man in a million,' as declared by the chairman of the occasion. Swamiji's reply was a masterpiece of oratory and patriotism as befitting the 'Prophet of Modern India'.

Swamiji said that he was the same Calcutta boy that the audience knew him as before his departure for the West, where the Parliament of Religions made an opening for him to reach first the American people, and then the English. He thanked the people of both these countries, and elaborated that the root cause of all the difficulties

between the Indians and the English was not 'knowing' each other. Speaking about Sri Ramakrishna, he referred to him as his Master and his God, and reiterated that while all the good acts emanated from his Master, the defective ones were his own, and forcefully declared that if India were to rise once again, then 'it will have to enthusiastically rally round his name'. He also stressed that, 'we can learn many things from the West, but the world is waiting for the treasure of our spirituality... therefore we must go out, exchange our spirituality for anything they have to give us... If you want to become equal with the Englishman or the American, you will have to teach as well as learn', and extolled the young Calcuttans to arise and awake to take India once more to her proper spiritual place.

Swamiji visited Dakshineswar on 7th March, the birth anniversary that year of Sri Ramakrishna. A vast sea of crowd of almost 60,000 people awaited him when he reached the Temple with his brother monks. But Swamiji first went to the Mother's temple, and then went around the temple on a pilgrimage with his European disciples. He met Girish Chandra Ghosh at the *panchvati*, the assemblage of five sacred trees, and also tried to give a unsuccessful speech to the yearning crowd, unsuccessfully though, for their shouts drowned his voice. Thereafter, he mingled with the crowd for some time, and then returned to the Alambazar *Math*.

Though Swamiji made his headquarters at the Seal's garden and the Alambazar *Math*, he frequently visited one or another devotee of the Master, and although people of all ages and vocations came to visit him, it was the youth who captivated his attention. He was consumed with the desire to infuse his own spirit in them, and wanted

to train the more energetic and serious among them. He rebuked them for their physical weaknesses, denounced early marriage, and castigated them for their lack of faith in themselves and in their traditional culture and ideals. He urged them to come out from the hypnotized state that India had been in 'for the last thousand years or more' when all along they had believed when told that they were good-for-nothings. He assured them that he would teach them how to come out of that rut and would rouse in them the faith that they have infinite power, unbounded wisdom and indomitable energy, and that they can do wonders. But after this, they must go from town to town, from village to village, from door to door and awaken every Indian to 'manifest the Divinity within.' All that he said or did was with sincere love, and it endeared him to his audience, many of whom became his followers and disciples.

Name, fame and money could not change the simple *sanyasi* that Swamiji was. He was courteous to all, and treated the relatives of his Guru with the same veneration that he reserved for his Guru, but he remonstrated against duplicity and chivalry. Swamiji also imbibed in his brother-monks the importance of concern and service to others, and bade them to come out of their traditional passive attitude of seeking monkhood for self-realisation and their own *mukti*, or emancipation, and to actively organise themselves to teaching and preaching. He proclaimed his mission to create an order of *sanyasis* or monks in India, who would dedicate their lives for others, raise the conditions of lives of the masses through their service, and bring about a religious renewal by spreading the teachings of the Master, and he considered this to be the Master's will for them to carry out. Slowly, the brother-monks acquiesced to this mission of Swamiji, and for the first time even Swami Ramakrishnananda left the precincts of the *Math* and, at the behest of Swami Vivekananda, went to Madras to open a *Vedanta* centre there. Similarly,

Group at Gopal Lal Seal's house, Calcutta.
Swami Vivekananda standing fifth from left.

Swami Akhandananda went to Murshidabad — a town in Bengal itself, to start famine relief work there. Swamis Saradananda and Abhedananda were already in the West looking after the work started there by Swamiji. The other brother-monks also placed themselves at the disposal of Swamiji and were willing to be sent anywhere on any mission. As a result of such outward movements of the monks, many centres and *ashramas*, or hermitages, came up at various places, and relief centres were ever ready at times of calamities anywhere. Swamiji was also intensely occupied with the idea of moving the *Math* to a permanent site on the banks of the Ganges, and to found an organisation that would train his disciples and serve the people.

Swamiji was worn out with constant meetings and talking, and the doctors advised him six months of complete rest, which was not possible while staying in Calcutta. He was also diagnosed to have acquired diabetes which was hereditary in his family and advised strict control of his diet. Therefore, he left for Darjeeling on 8th March. While the Seviers had preceded him to the place, his present entourage consisted of Swamis Brahmananda, Trigunatitananda, Turiyananda, Yogananda, *Babu* Girish Chandra Ghosh, Goodwin, Dr. Turnbill, and his Madras disciples Alasinga, Narasimhacharya and Mudaliar. The Maharaja of Burdwan revered Swamiji greatly, and placed a portion of his palatial residence at Darjeeling at his disposal. At Darjeeling, Swamiji was happy walking the mountain paths, visiting the neighbourhood Buddhist monastery, conversing with the members of his party, and spending hours in meditation. On

receiving a telegram announcing the Raja of Khetri's departure for Calcutta to meet Swamiji, Swamiji reached Calcutta on 21st March to meet the Raja, who had already arrived in the city three days earlier.

The Raja — accompanied by the Nawab of Loharu and other members of his entourage from Rajasthan and a huge crowd of mostly the Marwari gentry of Calcutta — was at the Sealdah station to receive Swamiji, who was then taken in a procession to the Seth's house where the Raja was staying. In the afternoon, Swamiji took the Raja to the Dakshineswar temple, and on their way back visited the Alambazar *Math*. Swamiji spent the night with the Raja at the Seth's house, and returned to the *Math* the next day to leave for Darjeeling once again on 23rd March. The Raja left Calcutta soon after on the 26th.

In May that year, Raja Ajit Singh of Khetri and several other Indian Princes were to go to England to attend the Diamond Jubilee Celebrations of Queen Victoria, and the Raja wanted Swamiji to accompany him. But Swamiji's doctors restrained him from doing so. He was cautioned against exerting himself in any manner, and was counselled not even to engage in any deep or serious thought. Darjeeling was doing him good, but a month of idleness was already tiring him, and his friends and disciples had to coerce him to stay put. However, he could not possibly stop thinking about the downtrodden masses of India, and, even while convalescing, he wrote to his disciple Margaret Nobel in England to take up the cause of the *Tiyas* — a plebeian caste of the Malabar — with the English Parliament as the Indian Government had refused to interfere on the plea of non-interference in the internal administration of a native state. Similarly, he was constantly engrossed with establishing an organisation that was to help him in his mission.

After about six weeks of interrupted stay at Darjeeling, Swamiji left for Calcutta on 28th April. But he remained in Calcutta only for a week, after which he left for Almora, again for health reasons. However, before leaving Calcutta, he first initiated four young men, who had joined the *Math* sometime back and were already leading the life of *brahmacharya*, a religious student practicing celibacy, and then two more thereafter. Before initiating them, the Swami warned them that they will have to renounce everything for the sake of the Lord, and 'being the teacher of your fellow-men and devoted to the self within, you will have to live to attain freedom and for the good of the world.' Swamiji also laid down a set of rules for the *Math*, and although he said, 'Our main object is to transcend all rules and regulations,' yet he also stressed on good rules and regulations to change the natural bad tendencies existing within people. He advised morning and evening meditations and exercises, afternoon studies, and evening discourses on the basis of some or the other religious book.

On 1st May, Swamiji called a meeting of all the monastic and lay disciples of Sri Ramakrishna at Balaram *babu's* house, where he propounded the establishment of the Ramakrishna Mission; and at

Balaram Bose's house in Calcutta

(opp.): At Bosepara Lane, Calcutta 1897
(Left to right): Swamis Trigunatita, Shivananda, Vivekananda, Turiyananada, and Brahmananda;
Sitting on floor: Swami Sadananda

a second meeting on 5th May, resolutions were passed laying down the aims and objectives of the Mission and the principles by which the movement was to be guided. Whereas the aim of the *Sangha* or association, known as Ramakrishna Mission was to preach the truths as preached and practised by Sri Ramakrishna and to help others put these truths into practice, its objective was conceived as conducting in the right spirit the activities of the movement inaugurated by Sri Ramakrishna for the establishment of fellowship amongst the followers of different religions. The methods of actions to be adopted included training of men to make them competent teachers of knowledge, conducive to the material and spiritual welfare of the masses, promoting and encouraging arts and industries, and introducing and spreading *Vedantic* religious ideas as elucidated by the life of Sri Ramakrishna. Whereas the activities of the Mission in India would involve the establishment of *maths* and *ashrams* in different parts of India, its foreign department was entrusted with sending trained members of the Order to foreign countries to start *Vedanta* centres there in order to bring about a closer relation and better understanding between India and those countries. Anyone believing in the mission of Sri Ramakrishna, or sympathetic to the aims and objectives as laid down was eligible to become a member. Swami Vivekananda was the first General President of the Ramakrishna Mission, and Swamis Brahmananda and Yogananda became the first president and vice president of the Calcutta centre respectively. Various lay disciples were appointed to various other posts, including that of the Secretary. Regular meetings were held every Sunday afternoon at Balaram *babu's* place, in which some or the other Holy Scriptures was read or recited from. Swamiji saw in Sri Ramakrishna a principle, and resisted forming another sect for the spread of religion only. He brought out the humane side

Group photo taken at Belur Math, 1899.

of the Master's nature and message, and showed that renunciation and service could go hand in hand. He expounded his ideal of rousing his countrymen from *tamas* or inertia, and inspired them to stand on their feet with the help of *Karma Yoga*. For almost three years, the preaching and philanthropic work of the Mission was carried out from Balaram *babu's* residence, till Swamiji moved the *Math* to Belur in 1899, and handed over its management in 1901 to a board of Trustees, whereupon the Mission merged with the *Math*. However, in order to increase the efficiency of the growing scope and responsibilities of the *Math*, the Ramakrishna Mission was registered in 1909 as a separate organisation, and while the *Math* was to continue the training and maintenance of a band of *sanyasis* to carry out religious works, the Mission was entrusted with charitable activities. However, the governing body of the Mission consistsed of the Trustees of the *Math*, and there was a close association between the two, and both had their headquarters at Belur.

The hard work in England, and the heat of southern India had exhausted Swamiji, and although the stay at Darjeeling did him some good, the doctors were not happy with his health, and advised him some more rest at yet another hill station. So Swamiji took the opportunity to respond to the repeated invitations from the residents of Almora to visit them, and accompanied by some of his brother-monks and disciples, he left Calcutta on 6th May to join Swami Shivananda, Goodwin and Miss Müller, whom he had already despatched to Almora almost a month back. After halting at Lucknow for a day, Swamiji reached Kathgodam on the 9th, and was escorted to Almora by several of his local admirers and by Goodwin, who had come down to receive him and his party at Kathgodam. At Lodea, near Almora, a large crowd was waiting to receive Swamiji, and at their persistent request, Swamiji had to mount a well-decorated horse, and thus travelled to Almora in a grand procession.

The city of Almora was bedecked for the occasion. Ladies showered flowers and rice from windows and housetops as the procession inched through the multitude. A *shamiana* or canopy, was erected at the centre of the town, and it was decorated with banners, festoons and flowers to welcome the Swami formally. Every house was lit up for the occasion, and music played all along to give a memorable effect to the whole event which was witnessed by several thousand people. While the pundits read out the welcome addresses in Hindi and Sanskrit, Swamiji replied briefly, touching emotionally on the spiritual influence of the Himalayas on the Indians, and his long desire to spend his last days at its feet. Although here also, visitors mobbed him continuously, the cool Himalayan weather aided in the gradual improvement of his health. Around 18th May, Swamiji with some of the people who had come down from Calcutta, left for Dewaldhar, situated at the feet of the Pindari Glacier, where he put up at the place of a relative of Lala Badri Sah, his host at Almora. This place did wonders to Swamiji's health, and he soon felt 'exuberant health' had returned. During this time he wrote extensive letters to Mary Hale, Margaret Nobel and other foreign disciples, and also to his brother monks, especially to Swami Akhandananda congratulating him for his exemplary service to the people of Murshidabad.

Vivekananda was at Dewaldhar for almost a month and returned to Almora around the 20th June, by which time the rains had set in and had cooled the atmosphere considerably. Although his health improved, his mind was perturbed by the news of a disastrous earthquake, extending from Simla to Assam and down under as far as Madras. Further, the unfavourable utterances of the visiting American missionary Dr. J. H. Barrows — the erstwhile Chairman of the Parliament of Religions — at various places in India also disturbed Swamiji as they emanated from a person whose welcoming to India was initiated by Swamiji himself. He wrote

In Calcutta, 1897.

to Mary Hale expressing his resentment at Dr. Barrows' frustrations, but reiterated his contentment at worshipping 'the only God that exists, the only God I believe in, the sum total of all souls — and above all my God the wicked, my God the miserable, my God the poor of all races, of all species, is the especial object of my worship'.

It was around this time only that Swamiji realised that 'at best' he had 'three or four more years of life left', and 'got to unbreast whatever I have to say, without caring if it smarts some or irritates others… If I have to please the world, that will be injuring the world.' Two more controversies, concerning Swamiji's remarks about the Theosophists and the present degeneration of the Buddhists, arose which distressed his disciples and friends for some time. However, Swamiji was against any form of flattery and spoke from the conviction of his knowledge. He believed in 'acceptance, love, toleration for everything sincere and honest, but never for hypocrisy.' He proclaimed that from what he has learnt from his experience, he has more sympathy for the English missionaries in India than either the Theosophists or the Buddhists. However, the stories of the success of the meetings of Ramakrishna Mission in Calcutta, Swami Ramakrishnananda's zealous preaching of the *Vedanta* in Madras, Swami Akhandananda's exemplary relief work at Murshidabad and Swami Saradanand's excellent work in America more than offset the disturbing effects of these biased controversies.

The first time Swamiji spoke in Hindi was at one of the two public lectures that he gave in Almora, and it was well received by the educated gentry of the town. Besides these, he also spoke at the English Club on 28th July, in which his discussions on tribal worship, the *Vedas*, and the relation of the soul to God, had the audience mesmerised.

It was at Almora that Swamiji heard from Mr. Sturdy from England that Margaret Nobel wished to come to India to help him in his work. Swamiji wrote to her saying that India needed a lioness to work for her women and he added, 'Your education, sincerity, purity, immense love, determination, and above all, the Celtic blood make you just the woman wanted.' But he also warned her of the immense difficulties that she would have to face in handling the deep rooted misery, superstition and slavery of half-naked men and women who shun the white skin because of fear and hatred, and a fearfully hot climate. However, Swamiji assured her that in spite of all this if she still decided to join him, he would always be beside her irrespective of her success or failure in her work. Thus reassured, Margaret Nobel came to India in early 1898.

After about three months' stay, Swamiji left Almora on 2nd August, and reached Bareilly on the 9th. He was given a warm welcome, and was able to convince a gathering of students to form a students' society that would extend *Vedantism* and do social service. He left Bareilly on 12th August and reached Ambala the next morning. Here too, a large crowd awaited him at the station, and Swamiji was taken to the bungalow that had been arranged for his stay, in a horse-drawn carriage. At Ambala, besides giving the usual discourses and lectures there, he also heeded to the request of a professor of the Lahore College and recorded a short lecture on a phonograph. He made it a point to visit the Hindu-Muslim School, which was symbolic of the spirit of unity of the two great Indian communities. Here he was also reunited with the Seviers who came there after their visit to Simla. His association with the Arya Samaj also began at Ambala. He received a mail from Mrs. Bull and Josephine McLeod from America expressing their willingness to come to India, and while welcoming them, he warned them on similar lines as he did Miss Nobel of England. In the mean time he also heard news of the English chapter not doing well and, therefore, Swami Abhedananda was sent to America. He asked Swami Saradananda to come back to India. Accordingly,

Mrs. Bull, Miss McLeod and Swami Saradananda reached India in early 1898.

Although it seemed as if Swamiji had recovered sufficiently at Almora, he was not as healthy as he appeared, and started getting frequent attacks of fever after reaching the plains. However, he continued with his mission of spreading his Master's words to different cities, and reached his next destination, Amritsar, on 20th August. His host, Todar Mall, a barrister-at-law, was worried about his deteriorating health and sent him to his friend's place at the nearby hill station of Dharamsala. Here Swamiji recuperated for about a week before returning to Amritsar around 28th August. Before leaving for another hill station, Muree, near Rawalpindi, on the 31st, he once again held religious discussions with the *Arya Samajists* at Amritsar. Swamiji was at Muree for a very short period, and left for Srinagar on 6th September, reaching there by boat from Baramula.

At Srinagar, Swamiji was the guest of Justice Rishibar Mukherjee. He also paid an informal visit to the palace, where Raja Ram Singh, the Maharaja's brother sat at his feet listening to him. Swamiji attended many private and public engagements, and visited the many attractive and historically important places across the valley before returning on 8th October to Muree, where a welcome address was presented to him on the 14th by the Punjabi and Bengali residents of the place. On 16th October, Swamiji left for Rawalpindi, and the following day he delivered a lecture to a large audience at Sardar Sujan Singh's garden. He stayed at Rawalpindi for two or three days, but had a hectic routine from early morning till late at night. He visited the Kali temple there several times. On receiving an invitation from the Maharaja of Kashmir to visit his state once again, Swamiji left Rawalpindi on the 20th for Jammu, where he stayed till the 29th. During this time he gave several public and private lectures.

In Kashmir sitting on chairs (Left to right): Swamis Sadananda, Vivekananda, Niranjananda, and Dhirananda.

(opp.): In a houseboat in Kashmir, 1898
(Left to right): Miss MacLeod, Swami Vivekananda, Mrs. Ole Bull and Sister Nivedita.

He had a long personal interview with the Maharaja on the 24th, during which he related the gradual decaying of social values in India, dwelt on his preaching of the *Vedanta* in Europe and America, pronounced the importance of foreign travel for the completion of one's education and also spoke about his mission.

His next destination was Sialkot, whence he reached Lahore on 5th November, where the Arya Samajists also awarded him a formal welcome. The high mark of his visit to Lahore was a lecture to a gathering of students from the four colleges of the city. He spoke to them on the monistic philosophy and religion of India and of love being the basis of *Adwaita*, which stressed on the presence of the same Lord everywhere. Swamiji succeeded in bringing about peace between the warring Arya Samajists and the Sanatanists of Punjab. He even suggested a method for rooting out the antagonism between the Arya Samajists and the Muslims, and endeavoured to irrigate the hearts of the people of Punjab, the land of the five rivers, with *bhakti*. Swamiji had a ready disciple in Sri Tirtha Ram Goswami — a professor of mathematics at one of the Lahore colleges — who later became Swami Ram Tirtha and busied himself with the spread of *Vedanta* in India and America. At Lahore, Swamiji also came across a childhood friend, Motilal Bose, who was now the owner of Prof. Bose's Circus in

Lahore, where Swamiji had given his second public lecture. After ten days' stay at Lahore, he left for Dehradun on 15th November. Swamiji's visit to Dehradun was once again on health grounds, and he preferred a secluded life here. But once the people came to know of his presence, they started turning up in large numbers and he spoke to them on religious matters.

Raja Ajit Singh had sent a personal emissary to Dehradun to take Swamiji to Khetri. Thus, Swamiji and party left Dehradun on 26th November and proceeded to Rajputana via Saharanpur, Delhi, and Alwar, where he was given a grand reception and met his friends and disciples from his days as a monk. From Alwar, he went to Jaipur where he put up at the same guest house of the Raja of Khetri where he had stayed earlier, as a wanderer, during which time he was considered more of a 'trouble' to the servants than a holy man. This time he was made to sleep on the Raja's bed, and thus observed 'it is the status of the man that is worshipped, not the body, nor the *Atman* within.' Travelling through the desert, Swamiji's party reached Khetri around 10th December, and was brought there in a procession by the Raja himself from a place twelve miles into the desert. At Khetri, he was treated like God's own child, and people prostrated before him and gave him offerings. At the official reception the Raja presented him with five trays full of gold *mohurs*, most of which he presented to the educational institutions of the state itself. On 20th December, Swamiji gave a public lecture on *Vedantism* to a gathering consisting of the elite of the kingdom and some Europeans. He paid high tributes to the Raja who as a true *kshatriya*, had assisted him materially in spreading *dharma* or the Eternal Truths of Hinduism, in the West. On his return journey from Khetri, the Raja accompanied Swamiji up to Jaipur, where they reached on 24th December.

Swamiji sent back from Jaipur to the *Math* in Calcutta all, but one of his entourage. He himself left for Khandwa on 1st January 1898. En route, he stayed at Jodhpur for about ten days. When he reached Khandwa he was already running a high fever, but his host and old acquaintance Haridas Chatterjee took good care of him, and he was soon on his feet. Due to his unsteady health, Swamiji had to abandon his plans of touring Sindh and Gujrat, and proceeded straight for Calcutta after about a week's stay at Khandwa.

The *Math* and the Missionaries

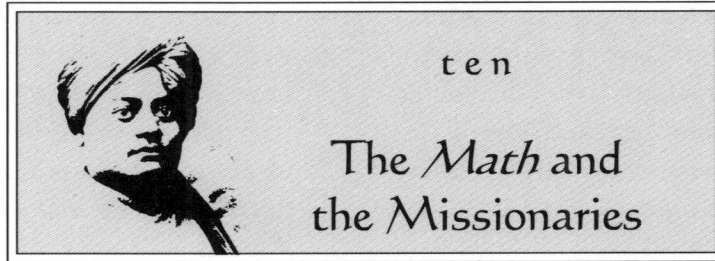

Swami Vivekananda reached Calcutta towards the end of January 1898, and stayed there for the next two months; busying himself visiting devotees, receiving visitors, training *sanyasis* and *brahmacharis*, and writing. He took regular classes on the scriptures; spoke about the *Upanishads*, the *Gita*, material sciences and the history of the nations; answered questions from the members of the *Math*; and taught them what he had learnt from his Master.

Margaret Nobel arrived in Calcutta on 28th January, and Swamiji went to receive her. It was thirteen months since they had last met. Initially, she put up at a friend's home on Park Street, and after the return of Miss Müller from Almora, the two shifted to a house at 34 Beniapukur Road. Swamiji trained the two, giving them a comprehensive understanding of Hindu culture, and guiding them towards their objective of establishing an institution for educating Indian women. Mahendra Nath Gupta, a disciple of Sri Ramakrishna, was entrusted with teaching her Bengali. Other visitors included Ole Bull of Boston and Josephine McLeod of New York who reached Calcutta on 14th February the same year.

On 6th February, Swamiji consecrated the shrine of Sri Ramakrishna at Nabagopal Ghosh's house at Ramakrishnapore in Howrah on the other side of the Ganges. After landing at the Ramkrishnapore *ghat* or the wharf, Swamiji personally led the chorus and headed the procession from the *ghat* to Ghosh's house. The people were thoroughly impressed by the Swami's humble ways and regal bearing. Swamiji himself was elated to see the porcelain figure of Sri Ramakrishna on the throne of the marble floored worship-room of the Ghoshs and assured the lady of the house that the Master would definitely reside here 'with all these services of devoted hearts.' He then smeared himself with ashes and invoked the presence of Sri Ramakrishna with the salutation 'O Ramakrishna, the Reinstator of Religion, the Embodiment of all Religions, the Greatest of all Incarnations,' while his disciple, Swami Prakashananda, recited the prescribed *mantras*.

In March, Swamiji bought a building on a seven-acre plot of land at Belur on the west bank of the Ganges. Miss Henrietta Müller had donated the entire amount of Rs. 39,000 for the purchase of the property, on which was to come up the long cherished temple of Sri Ramakrishna and the headquarters of the Order. Swami Vigyanananda, an erstwhile Executive Engineer with the government of the then North-Western Provinces, (now Uttar Pradesh) was entrusted with the supervision of the construction work of the temple, while Swami Adwaitanand assisted him in the supervision of the preparatory work. A handsome contribution of a lakh of rupees from Mrs. Ole Bull enabled the construction of the shrine and the prayer hall, along with a kitchen, store and refectory in the basement, which took a year to complete. Swamiji created an endowment with the remaining money. The monastery came to be known as Belur *Math*, and it became the permanent headquarters of the Ramakrishna Order from January 1899 onwards. In the meantime, in February 1898, the *Math* was shifted from the 1897 earthquake affected Alambazar property to Nilambar Mukherjee's garden-house, only a furlong away from the construction site of the Belur *Math*. After repairing the old house in the newly purchased plot, Mrs. Bull and Miss McLeod shifted there in March 1898 and Margaret Nobel joined them soon after. They were there for almost two months, during which time Swamiji would come every morning and have tea under the mango tree in front of the house. He would spend hours teaching them about Indian history, folklore, and society in a vivid, poetic and dramatic way, and explained to them the intricacies of Hindu religious ideals, forms of worship and outlook on life. They learned the great ideals and watchwords of the Indian ethos and became one with it, and all differences of knowledge of the

Sri Ramakrishna temple, Belur Math.

(opp.): Facimile of pages of a poem written by Sri Ramakrishna.

eastern and western disciples vanished. It was not an easy job, but Swamiji was aware of his responsibility of acclimatising his foreign disciples — who come from different backgrounds — with the spirituality and poverty of Indian life.

The *Shivaratri* festival preceded Sri Ramakrishna's birthday by three days, and the *Math* was now full. All the monks had come back after being successful in their respective work. Swami Saradananda had returned from America, Swami Shivananda from Ceylon, and Swami Trigunatitananda from Dinajpur after finishing the famine relief work there. Swami Akhandananda had also come from his orphanage at Murshidabad.

Swamiji congratulated Brahmananda for the success of the Mission under his guidance, and Turiyananda for training the young *sanyasis* and *brahmacharis* during the absence of Swamiji himself. A thanksgiving night was held on *Shivatatri* where the young *sanyasis* and *brahmacharis* read out addresses of thanks to all the senior Swamis, and they replied in turn. The sixty-fifth birth anniversary of Sri Ramakrishna was celebrated at the *Math* with great fanfare on 22nd February under the supervision of Swamiji himself, and the evening *aarti* song *Khandana-bhava-bandhana*, composed by Swamiji himself, was sung for the first time. However, the venue for the public celebration of the Master's birthday had to be shifted that year from Dakshineswar — where it had been held every year since 1881, that is, when the Master was still alive — to Purnachandra Daw's *Radharamanji Thakurbari* at Bally as the trustees of the Kali Temple objected to the presence of Swamiji's western disciples on the occasion. The celebration took place on 27th February at the new venue with great fervour and the usual impressiveness.

Swamiji made few public appearances during this period of stay in Calcutta. But on 11th March, he presided over a meeting at Star Theatre, as arranged by the Ramakrishna Mission for Margaret Nobel's rendition of her treatise entitled *The Influence of Indian Spiritual Thought in England*. Swamiji introduced her as 'another gift from England', the others being Henrietta Müller and Annie Besant, all of whom had 'consecrated their lives to the good of India'. Miss Müller and Mrs. Bull, both of whom were present there, also spoke on the occasion. The next meeting that Swamiji presided over in Calcutta was held on 18th March at the Emerald Theatre. Here Swami Saradananda spoke on *Our Mission in America*. Among those present that day were Dr. Jagadish Chandra Bose of Calcutta, and the Honourable Rai A. Charlu Bahadur of Madras.

On the morning of 25th March, Swamiji went to the cottage at Belur where the three western ladies were staying, and brought them to the *Math*, which was at that time temporarily situated in the neighbour, Neelambar *babu's*, garden house. He took Miss Nobel to the shrine-room, and taught her the worship of Lord Shiva. Then Swamiji went through a simple ritual of initiation, and Margaret Nobel became a *brahmacharini*. She was given the name Nivedita, meaning one who is dedicated. Later she became famous as Sister Nivedita both in India and abroad. Another event that occurred around the same time was the initiation of Swamis Sureshwarananda and Swarupananda on 29th March. Swami Swarupananda was an excellent

worker and Swamiji initially made him the editor of the *Prabudha Bharat*, and later on he became the President of the Adwaita *Ashram* when it was founded in Mayavati, near Almora, early next year.

Swamiji's intensive training of his western disciples took up the whole of 1898. As he moved from city to city, and from province to province with them, he recounted the glories and beauties of the land, and also gave them a clear understanding of the problems to which they could apply ideals and methods of western science and civilisation. The training shaped their lives irrevocably, and made them apostles of Hinduism.

On 30th March, Swamiji left for a short stay at Darjeeling. Swami Nirbhayananda and Nityagopal Bose accompanied him, and Swamiji tried his best to follow the doctor's advice of not thinking on any serious subject. However, he responded to the requests of the local residents, and on 3rd April he gave a lecture on Hinduism at the Darjeeling Hindu Public Hall. Miss Müller and Swami Akhandanand reached Darjeeling on 7th April. Swamiji also visited Sandakphu to see the snow, and on returning to Darjeeling he had a bout of fever, cough and cold. He had recuperated only partially when the news of the outbreak of plague in Calcutta reached him. He became very remorseful and declared, 'We have to serve them, even though we are required to sell everything. We were only wandering monks living under a tree. We shall stay under a tree.'

People were terror-stricken and fleeing Calcutta in panic. Troops had to be called in to quell riots. Swamiji reached Calcutta on 3rd May to be of help to his people. He understood the gravity of the situation and planned immediate relief operations. A big plot of land was taken on rent, and segregated camps were set up there. He instructed volunteers to teach the people about sanitation and to clean the lanes and houses of their respective areas of activities. Such activities soon brought the plague under control and people got back their confidence and returned to Calcutta.

Swamiji remained in Calcutta once the situation turned for the better and the stringent plague regulations were withdrawn.

In the meantime, Mr. and Mrs. Sevier had settled down in Almora, and were asking Swamiji to go there to recuperate fully. Accordingly, Swamiji left Calcutta on 11th May with a big party comprising the Swamis Turiyananda, Niranjananda, Sadananda and Swarupananda, and Mrs. Bull, Sister Nivedita, Miss McLeod and the American Consul-General's wife Mrs. Patterson, whom Swamiji knew from America. They reached Kathgodam by train and from there they took carriages and *dundies* (a crude variety of palanquin used to carry people up the hilly terrains) upto Nainital. En route, Swamiji enlightened the party with the history, importance and the topography of the places through which the train went — Patna, Varanasi, Lucknow, the Terai region, the arid lands and the plains — and took the opportunity to apprise the westerners about the religious rites and rituals. Swamiji's vivid and indulging descriptions once again echoed his much repeated saying, 'India I loved before I came away; now the very dust of India has become holy to me, the very air is now to me holy; it is now the holy land, the place of pilgrimage, the *tirtha*.'

Some disciples of Swami Vivekananda at Mayavati
Top row (left to right): Swamis Prakashananda, Swarupananda, and Sacchidananda
Bottom row (left to right): Mrs. Sevier, Swamis Nirbhayananda, Virajananda, Vimalananda, and Brahmachari Amritananda.

During this time, the Raja of Khetri was camping in Nainital. So after reaching the place on 13th May, the party halted there for a couple of days before proceeding to Almora, just thirty-two miles (about 51 km) away. A warm reception was given to Swamiji at Nainital. Here he also met a Muslim, Mohammad Sarfraz Hussain, who believed that the Swami was an avatar, a prophet, and became his disciple, taking the name Mohammedananda. He was deeply influenced by Swamiji's *Adwaitism*, or monistic *Vedantism* that looked upon all religions and sects with love.

Swamiji and his party left for Almora on 16th May and after making their way through dense forests on the hills, they reached Almora the next morning. Swamiji, his disciples, and his brother-monks were the guests of the Seviers, while the western ladies put up at the nearby Oakley House. Swamiji used to go for an early morning walk and then would breakfast with the ladies at Oakley House and after that he would sit with them conversing on any and every aspect of India and the world. It was in Almora that Swamiji personally Indianised his spiritual daughter Sister Nivedita to prepare her for the work that she was to do for this

country and its womenfolk. At Almora, Swamiji met many of its residents, and also some visitors, including Annie Besant and Aswini Kumar Dutta, the saintly patriot of Bengal. The police of Almora also kept watch on the Swami's movements, and those of Sister Nivedita, who had had some earlier association with the Irish revolutionaries. At Almora, Swamiji retired for a few days to Shiyadevi, a lonely place situated some distance from the town. He was happy to prove to himself once again that his sojourn in the West could not take away the spirit of the true *sanyasi* in him, and that he could still wander bare-foot, endure cold and heat and meditate alone. On 30th May, he accompanied the Seviers for a week in a futile search for an estate that could function as a Himalayan monastery. He was also pained when he got the news of the deaths of Pawhari Baba, whom he loved 'second only to Sri Ramakrishna'; his American friend Mrs. Bagley; his companion and disciple Goodwin; and B.R. Rajam Iyer, the editor of *Prabuddha Bharat*, which was then published from Madras (it was shifted to Almora only after Rajam Iyer's death saw its closure there). The news of so many deaths saddened Swamiji a lot, and he decided to leave Almora for Kashmir.

Swamiji and party left Almora on 11th June and reached Kathgodam, via Bhim Tal, on the 14th. From Kathgodam they boarded a train for Punjab, and passing through Ludhiana, Lahore, and Rawalpindi, they reached Muree on 15th June and stayed there for three days. The party left Muree on the 18th and reached Srinagar via Uri and Baramula. Throughout the days of the journey from Almora to Srinagar, Swamiji pondered on various episodes of his life, on Hindu mythology, the *Vedas*, the *Upanishads*, his worship of Lord Shiva, and of course on the importance, history and topography of the places they passed through. The last leg of their journey was on houseboats, and these remained their residence from 22nd June till 15th July. There were many excursions through remain quite sane, taken side by side with the Indian notion that till a man had been alone for twenty years, he could not be regarded as perfectly himself. Swamiji's consideration for his disciples was exemplary and that year he celebrated the American independence day for his three American disciples by writing a poem 'To the Fourth of July'. The poem encompassed his own longing for the 'Final Freedom in the Infinite', which proved prophetic, as four years later he entered into Final Freedom or *mahasamadhi*, on that very day. Such was his desire for peace and solitude that he even made an abortive attempt to reach Amarnath from Gulmarg via Sonmarg.

On 19th July, the party left Srinagar for Anantnag, and on its way, visited the old temple of Pandrethan, which served as a perfect example for Swamiji to explain Indian architecture and archaeology to his western disciples. The arches, sculptures and friezes had definite influence of Buddhism, one of the four religious periods that

pristine natural surroundings and the several discourses held by Swamiji made the four western ladies accompanying him, experience an unparalleled educational wisdom. Their day-to-day experiences were also very enriching; like the one they had when they visited Kheer Bhawani and the Muslim boatman would not allow them to land there with their shoes on.

Often Swamiji would break away from his companions and roam about in solitude, and then return radiant and rejuvenated. The western disciples were reminded of the difference between eastern and western methods of thought through the drastic example of the European idea that a man could not live alone for twenty years and

Near the Amarnath cave.
(right): Ice-linga, Amarnath cave.

(opp.): Kshir Bhavani Temple, Kashmir.

In Kashmir
(left to right): Miss MacLeod, Mrs. Ole Bull,
Swami Vivekananda and Sister Nivedita.

Kashmir has gone through, the other three being tree and snake worship from which evolved the names of the springs ending in 'nag'; Hinduism, in the form of Sun worship; and Mohammedanism. They next came across the two great temples of Avantipore, and here also the Swami spoke about *Adwaita Vedanta* as the mother of all religions, and also about the future of India. They reached Anantnag on 22nd July, and the following day they visited the ruins of Martand. On 25th July they went to Achabal and roamed in the gardens built by Emperor Jehangir, then they bathed in a pool opposite Pathan Khan's *zenana* and had lunch in the garden.

Swamiji and Sister Nivedita joined the Amarnath pilgrims from Anantnag, and the others waited at Pahalgam for their return. Leaving Anantnag on 26th July, the entourage reached Pahalgam on the 28th where they halted for a day before Swamiji and Sister Nivedita resumed their journey to Amarnath on the 30th. During this pilgrimage, Swamiji observed all religious rites and customs zealously, and practised all austerities with devotion. He introduced Sister Nivedita to the group of devotees travelling together to Amarnath by having her distribute alms to them and take their blessings. Swamiji's liberal views on religious matters, and his love and sympathy for Islam attracted many people to his tent, and Sister Nivedita's amiable manners soon endeared her to the pilgrims. Passing through Seshnag at Mahaguru's Top, a pass at 14,500 feet, and Panchtarani, the 'place of five streams' at 12,500 feet, they reached Amarnath on 2nd August. Swamiji bathed in a stream flowing before the ascent to the cave. He smeared his body with ashes, and entered the cave, 'his face aflame with devotion to Shiva' and his whole frame shaking with emotion. Never had Swamiji experienced such spiritual exaltation as in visiting the Amarnath shrine, where he was face to face with Lord Shiva. So enthralled was Swamiji in the presence of Shiva that he could speak of nothing else for days after his visit to the caves. Even after returning to Pahalgam and meeting the other western disciples there, he spoke about Shiva and the cave, and the great vision. After the party returned to Srinagar from Pahalgam, on 8th August via Anantnag, Mrs. Patterson joined her husband who was visiting Srinagar, while the others remained there till the end of September.

Although Swamiji's longing for solitude grew after the visit to Amarnath, and he would often drift away in his boat and remain alone for days, he continued with his instructions for his disciples on the inclusiveness of the country and its religions, on making Hinduism more active and aggressive, on the necessity of blending the highest meditative life with the most active, and its practice. The Maharaja of Kashmir, who had met Swamiji earlier and was greatly impressed by him, treated Swamiji and his party well, and various high officials visited his houseboat for religious and other general discourses. The Maharaja even donated a plot of land where Swamiji could establish a monastery and a Sanskrit school, but the English Resident vetoed it.

Swamiji's departure from Srinagar was delayed due to the severe deterioration of his health on account of his frequent exertions in the mountains. He had an enlargement of heart. However, his devotion to the Mother increased, and he even performed the *Kanya Kumari* worship of the four-year-old daughter of his Muslim boatman. He could intensely feel the constant presence of the Mother, and even had a repetition of the blissful experience that he had had at the Dakshineswar Temple when he had gone to pray to Mother Kali on the insistence of his Master. After this experience,

Swamiji retired to Kheer Bhawani on 30th September, with strict instructions to be left alone, and returned only on 6th October. Even thereafter, he practiced the sternest austerities as if to tear off the resultant layers of years of work and thought, and to again be a child before the Divine Mother.

Swamiji longed to go back to Calcutta and was waiting for the arrival of Swami Saradananda to whom he had written in August to come to Kashmir. After the arrival of the latter and once Swamiji was somewhat fit to travel, the whole party left for Baramula by boat, which they reached on or around 11th October. Leaving his entourage in the care of Swami Saradananda, Swamiji left for Rawalpindi all by himself, on his way back to Calcutta via Lahore.

Swamiji reached the *Math* — still at Nilambar Mukherjee's garden house at Belur — on 18th October. He looked pale and was ill, and on reaching the monastery, took to his bed almost immediately. He was suffering from asthma and a blood clot had developed in his left eye. Once the news of his illness spread, devotees started gathering at the *Math*, but he rarely spoke to anybody, and confined himself to his room. However, he spoke at length of his experiences at Amarnath and Kheer Bhawani to his disciple Sarat Chandra Chakrabarty. In spite of his health, Swamiji soon resumed his old ways at the *Math*, and went about earnestly in religious conversations, scripture classes, and training the members of the *Math* with all seriousness. To facilitate his treatment, from November 1898 onwards, Swamiji kept alternating the place of residence between the monastery at Belur and Balaram *babu's* house in Calcutta. In spite of his brother-monks trying to bring about some routine in his daily meetings, Swamiji continued meeting the many people who flocked to meet him at all hours. He was an embodiment of love, and would bless anyone who came to him, irrespective of his previous life or inner propensities.

On the parameters of Hinduism his views were simple but profound. He said, 'The Hindu must not give up his religion, but must keep religion within its proper limits and give freedom to society to grow.' He possessed a strong revulsion against casteism, and would say, 'Caste is simply a crystallised social institution which after its service is now filling the atmosphere of India with its stench, and it can only be removed by giving back to the people their lost social individuality ... Every man born in India knows that he is a slave of society. Now, freedom is the only condition of growth; take that off, the result is degeneration.' Swamiji would say, 'I disagree with all those who are giving their superstitions back to my people... My hope is to see again the strong points of that India (India of one's books, one's studies, one's dreams), reinforced by the strong points of this age, only in a natural way. The new state of things must be a growth from within. So I preach only the *Upanishads*... And of the *Upanishads*, it is only that one idea — strength. The quintessence of *Vedas* and *Vedanta* — all lies in that one word.' He loved to dwell on the spectacle of the historical emergence of Hinduism, and sought the great force behind the evolution of any phenomenon. He would query, 'Where was the thinker behind the founder of a religion, and where was the heart to complete the thought?' Buddha had received his philosophy of the five essentials — form, feeling, sensation, motion and knowledge — from Kapil *muni,* and Buddha introduced the love that made the philosophy live; but his theory of non-injury provoked weakness. On the other hand, Krishna's philosophy as enshrined in the *Gita* is strong and beautiful, and rouses the spirit of the *Puranas,* the ancient Holy Scriptures. Swamiji delved that at any given time in the growth of Hinduism, there have always been several sects propounding the realisation of God through all gradation of means: from that of using the senses as an instrument for achieving Him, to that of annihilation of the senses,

again to achieve Him. 'At the present moment, we may see three different positions of the national religion — the Orthodox, the Arya Samaj and Brahmo Samaj. The Orthodox covers the ground taken by the Vedic Hindus of the *Mahabharat* epoch. The Arya Samaj corresponds with Jainism, and the Brahmo Samaj with the Buddhists.' Swamiji considered Buddhism as reformed Jainism, which practised the slow destruction of the body itself by self-torture.

In the meantime, Sister Nivedita returned to Calcutta on 1st November, and went straight to Swamiji's place at Baghbazar. Swamiji arranged for her stay with Mother Sarada, who was also staying at the nearby address of 10/2 Bosepara Lane. Although the Mother had taken Sister Nivedita to her heart, there were complaints from the old orthodox ladies staying with her, and Nivedita soon moved out to the house at 16 Bosepara Lane, where she lived till she left for the West in June 1899. Mrs. Bull and Miss McLeod returned to Calcutta on 6th November and they stayed with Sister Nivedita at her new residence for some time. It was during this time that Mrs. Bull could persuade the Holy Mother to consent to her photograph being taken, for her to take back to America. On 12th November, the Holy Mother went to bless the Belur *Math,* and on Kali Puja the next day she also blessed the occasion of the ceremonial opening of Sister Nivedita's girls' school at Baghbazar.

Towards the end of November 1898, Sir Jamshedji Tata — who had known the Swami since July 1893 when they had travelled together from Yokohama to Chicago — wrote to Swamiji requesting him to start a crusade on the channelising of the ascetic spirit of India for the cultivation of natural and humanistic sciences. This had been the driving force behind his humble scheme of Research Institute of Science for India. Whereas the consecration of the land for the new *Math* was done in March 1898, the consecration of the *Math* itself was done in an impressive ceremony on Friday, 9th December 1898. Swamiji himself performed all the rites, and was helped by the brother-monks and his disciples. The urn containing the ashes of Sri Ramakrishna was brought in a grand procession from Nilambar Mukherjee's garden house by Swamiji who recollected his Master's saying 'I will go and live wherever it will be your pleasure to take me, carrying me on your shoulders be it under a tree or in the humblest cottage', and himself added, 'so long as his name inspires his followers with his ideals of purity, holiness, and loving charity to all men, even so long shall he, the Master, sanctify the place with his hallowed presence.' The rites over, Swamiji spoke to the gathering, expressing his desire that the *punyakshetra*, or holy place, should become 'a unique centre of the harmony of all the different religions and sects, for the good of the Many, for the happiness of the Many'. The celebrations ended with the return procession to the adjoining old *Math,* or Nilambar Mukherjee's garden house.

It was on 2nd January 1899 that the *Math* was finally moved to its new premises. Swamiji visualised the *Math* as the central institution of a religious university involved in the practice of religion and the cultivation of knowledge, the spiritual force emanating from which will permeate the whole world. He planned to re-introduce the *gurukul* system of in-house learning for prospective *brahmacharis* who would then have the option of either returning to their homes after the five year course or join the *Math*. Swamiji also envisaged the acquisition of the adjoining land on the south of the *Math* and construct an *annasatra* or gruel kitchen, to feed the *daridra* Narayana by the trained *brahmacharis* who will have to find the means to support it if necessary even by begging from door to door. It is only after the *brahmacharis* complete their services thus, that they would be entitled to enter the *sanyas ashram* after due initiation by the *Math*. The President would have the power to waive this rule for specially gifted *brahmacharis* and initiate them any time. The *Math* would thus be involved in the religion of Man-making by harmonising the three aspects of *annadan*, or the giving of food and other necessities of physical life; next *vidyadan*, or the imparting of intellectual knowledge; and last *gyanadan*, or the conferring of spiritual knowledge. *Sanyasis* passing through all these three phases will then strive to exemplify the truth of pure *Adwaita* in practical life, bringing it out from the forests and mountain caves and spreading it to everyday society and the world. Swamiji would say that *gyan, bhakti* and *shakti* are present in every man, it is only in the degree of manifestation that makes one great and another small; and once perfection is reached in the harmony of these three in any man, then he succeeds in achieving whatever he wants, whatever he wishes. He advocated the principle of practical *Vedanta,* of sharing the

knowledge of *Adwaita* with the whole universe and thereby achieving the bliss of seeing oneself in every human being, rather than utilising it for one's own *mukti* alone. Swami Vivekananda would say that, 'He alone is a child of Sri Ramakrishna who is moved to pity for all creatures and exerts himself for them even at the risk of personal damnation. Whoever, at this great spiritual juncture, will stand up with a courageous heart and go on spreading from door to door, from village to village, his message is alone my brother and a son of his. This is the test, he who is Ramakrishna's child does not seek his personal goal.'

Swamiji left for Baidyanathdham on 19th December, and was the guest of Priyanath Mukherjee. Swamiji spent most of the time by himself, in reading, writing and by going for long walks. He was not well at all, and acquired an acute form of asthma, from which he almost suffocated one day. His condition worsened towards the middle of January 1899, and Swamis Saradananda and Sadananda reached Deoghar to bring him back as soon as his health would permit the return travel.

The *Karma Yogi* that he was, Swamiji would work as long as he could, and he kept up his illuminating correspondences with his disciples even amidst his sickness. In one of his letters from Deoghar to a lady disciple, Mrinalini Bose, Swamiji explained the concept of prevention of widow remarriage amongst the higher classes very lucidly. He said that it was more of a social necessity that brought about the custom amongst the higher classes, which had greater number of women than men. Thus, society prevented a widow — who has already had her share of a married life — from remarrying which would otherwise deprive a maiden from having a husband. He pointed out that for the same reason, in lower classes or in communities that had a greater number of men than women, widow remarriage was allowed since the situation here was just the reverse. He asserted that this is true for all social follies, and it is necessary to first alter the situation that gives rise to such follies, for example, the caste system, since this will make the custom die on its own.

Swamiji's dream of starting a Bengali publication from Calcutta eluded him for quite some months. It was made possible only after the purchase of a press with the eight hundred dollars that Miss Josephine McLeod donated to Swamiji after her return to Calcutta from North India. Thus, the first issue of the *Udbodhan* came out on 14th January 1899. Swami Trigunatitanand volunteered to be the editor and manager of the journal which envisaged publishing positive ideas for the physical, mental and spiritual improvement of the readers, simple disseminations of the highest doctrines of the *Vedas* and *Vedantas* that could help raise the *chandal* reader to attain the status of a *brahmin* and spreading the message of universal harmony as preached by Sri Ramakrishna.

Swamiji returned to Calcutta on the night of 22nd January 1899, and was feeling much better. By February, Swamiji was back full-fledged in his work of training at the *Math*. He demanded exactness from the monks so that they might learn attentiveness and accuracy, which were so very essential to become a perfect *sanyasi*. In order to encourage the students, Swamiji would extol even the smallest of their accomplishments and would always encourage their performances. He was happy the way the *Math* work was being administered by Swami Saradananda, and delegated the responsibilities of the day-to-day affairs to the younger members, who elected a superintendent from amongst themselves every month. Swamiji thus, immersed himself wholeheartedly in the building of the monastic order.

Swamiji would advise the monks to practise intense *tapasya* or meditation, self-control and concentration to succeed, and ask them to prepare themselves as fit agents for God's work. He would invigorate them to believe in themselves even before believing in God, and remind them that the history of the world is the history of a few men who had faith in themselves. Swamiji told them that only a great monk can be a great worker but prompted that the *gerua* (ochre) robe is not for enjoyment, rather it is the banner for heroic work. He counselled them to give their body, mind and spirit to the welfare of the society. 'Let your God be the poor, the illiterate and the ignorant, and serve them as you would serve God,' and advocated this service to man to encompass feeding of the poor, nursing the sick, relief during famine, supervising sanitation during epidemics, and founding orphanages, hospitals and centres of education and training. He prescribed physical exercises as a must for all the disciples, and said that he wanted 'sappers and miners in the army of religion,' He believed that 'well developed bodies, muscles of iron and nerves of steel' were required for the type of work that the Mission was to be involved in. But he also stressed on the importance of study to develop well-reasoned judgement on the social and spiritual needs of the time and their mutual adjustment, and to bring about an exchange of the highest ideals between the East and the West. Swamiji would tell them, 'Service and not mercy should be your guiding principles…*Karma* is religion and religion is *Karma. Karma* leads man to God.'

Swamiji would continuously impress on his monastic disciples the salutary importance of renunciation and unbroken *brahmacharya* for the realisation of the 'Highest'. He insisted on strict discipline and observation of the regulations by the *brahmacharis*. He advocated a light dinner and was against over-eating for it ruined both the body and the mind. The *brahmacharis* had to rise early, be punctual about their daily routine, converse only on religious subjects. They were forbidden to even read the newspaper or have any liaison with the householders for a certain time during their training. However, he gave the disciples an open choice of returning to the householder's life anytime they found that they were not able to adhere to the high ideals and rigorous discipline of *sanyas*. He found this to be more desirable than leading a hypocritical life and bringing about disgrace to themselves and the order. Swamiji prohibited any interference of the 'men of the world' in the affairs of the *Math*, and forbade the *sanyasis* to pay respects to the rich and 'hang on them for support', which has been the bane of all monastic communities of India because 'such conduct becomes a public woman rather than one who professes to have renounced the world'.

Swamiji would say that if he had 'two thousand enthusiastic youths and three hundred million rupees' at his command, then he could solve all the problems of India and put her on her feet, and would sometimes be frustrated at not getting what he thus desired. 'However, I will do the very best of myself and infuse my spirit in others to continue the work. No rest for me. I shall die in harness…. let me live and die in action', and he expounded his disciples thus: 'Sri Ramakrishna came and gave his life for the world; I will also sacrifice my life, you also, everyone of you should do the same. All these works are only a beginning. Believe me, from the shedding of our life-blood will arise gigantic heroes and warriors of God, who will revolutionise the whole world.'

Many people came to the Swami from near and far, and discussions on religion and philosophy were a regular process. But one exceptional visitor was Nag Mahasay from Deobhog in Dacca, now in Bangladesh, who was an epitome of *Supreme Bhakti* and a great devotee of Sri Ramakrishna. He visualised Lord Shiva in Swamiji, and was oblivious even of himself. Swamiji was also very impressed by Nag Mahasay's understanding of Ramakrishna and invited him to come and stay at the *Math*, but Nag Mahasay humbly declined the offer stating, "I once asked the Master's permission to give up the world. He said, 'Live in the world.' So I am following his command …."

Swamiji told the monks that it was time for them to go out into the world and preach the gospel of Sri Ramakrishna, and in this direction, he instructed the two disciples Swamis Virajananda and Prakashananda to proceed to Dacca at once. They did so on 4th February 1899. Swamiji also sent Swamis Saradananda and Turiyananda to preach in Gujarat, and they left on the 7th. They returned after three months and Swamiji was elated to learn about their success. Swami Ramakrishnananda had also started a centre in Madras and had been successful in his teaching work there. Swami

Swami Abhedananda's work in the USA, particularly in New York where he settled down and began taking classes on yoga and meditation, was well appreciated by the local people, and many of his lectures got rave reviews in some of the best papers and journals there. Madam Marie Louise, or Swami Abhayananda as she came to be known after her initiation, also turned out to be a successful preacher of *Vedanta* in different parts of the United States, until on popular demand, she established the Adwaita Society in Chicago and settled down there.

Shivananda — whom Swamiji had deputed to work in Ceylon amongst the Tamils and Sinhalese — was not only successful in arousing interest in the *Vedanta* philosophy amongst the local people, he was also a successful teacher. He held classes on *Raja Yoga* and the *Gita*, which were attended by many locals and Europeans also; so much so that he initiated one Mrs. Pickett as Haripriya and trained her to teach the *Vedanta* and then sent her to Australia and New Zealand. She began taking classes in Adelaide and South Victoria in Australia, and Nelson in New Zealand.

The Seviers were also successful in giving shape to Swamiji's dream of opening a monastery in the cool, secluded region of the Himalayas. The chosen site was at the beautiful and scenic Mayavati estate at a height of 6,400 feet and some fifty miles east of Almora. The Adwaita *Ashram* was formally established here on 19th March 1899, the day on which the birth anniversary of Sri Ramakrishna was publicly celebrated that year. The *Prabuddha Bharat*

(left to right): Swami Abhedananda; Swami Shivananda; Swami Akhandananda.

was shifted and brought here. Swamiji set the principles of this *Ashram* as 'free from all superstitions and weakening contaminations,' and as one teaching only the 'Doctrine of Unity, pure and simple.' This *ashram* was exclusively dedicated to *Adwaita* and there was to be no external worship of God in the form of images, pictures, or symbols, in fact, not even the worship of Sri Ramakrishna, which was central to all other monastic centres of the Ramakrishna Order.

The *Brahmavadin* from Madras (it now comes out as *The Vedanta Kesari*), *Prabuddha Bharat* from Almora, and *Udbodhan* from Calcutta are the three magazines that were started with Swamiji's blessings, and all three helped in spreading Swamiji's mission in India and abroad. At present they help in the dissemination of the thoughts and ideals of the great ancient Indian sages and philosophers, issue reports of the activities of the Order, and publish the writings and lectures of the members.

Swami Akhandananda also progressed well with the educational work in Khetri in the state of Gujarat, where he virtually revolutionised the slave system that existed there, and freed many slave boys and arranged for their education. At the instance of Swami Vivekananda and with the Raja of Khetri's initiation and help, additional funds were made available for education and the local Sanskrit School was converted into a Vedic School. Swami Akhandananda also visited the holy place of Nathdwara in the Udaipur State and started a Middle English School there, which ran for some time with the help of a local Bengali youth. He was also successful in establishing cultural associations in Alwar and other princely states of Rajputana, and these associations were also involved with matters concerning the welfare of the people. Fired by his leader's moving spirit of the ideal of service to fellow-men, Swami Akhandananda was the first to put it into practice, and during his work with famine relief in Murshidabad he opened an orphanage for the deserted children of the famine-affected villages. He was involved in their all-round growth and he set about to 'make men' of them.

Swami Trigunatitananda opened another famine relief centre on the lines of the Murshidabad prototype at Dinajpur in August 1897. His work was much appreciated by both the government and the local residents. After the calamity was over the latter convened a public meeting to present an address of thanks to the Swami.

Relief centres were also opened in Deoghar, Dakshineswar and Calcutta as and when the need arose. The Ramakrishna Mission was very organized in the way it handled the plague in Calcutta in the year 1899. Sister Nivedita and Swami Sadananda led the plague service this time, and *bustees* in four areas of the city were cleared of cartloads of accumulated filth and thoroughly disinfected. To boost the morale of the people and encourage the workers, Swamiji also chose to live in the slums, and his stirring words found students volunteering for door-to-door inspection of huts in the *bustees*, or shantytown, for distribution of literature on sanitation, and for counselling.

Swamiji's concern for his countrymen spread beyond all regions, and he never missed an opportunity to enquire about or ponder on the sufferings of his brethren from and with the many visitors who came to him from all parts of the country. He observed that, 'Three things are necessary to make every man great, every nation great: 1) Conviction of the powers of goodness; 2) Absence of jealousy and suspicion; 3) Helping all who are trying to be and do good.' Unfortunately, he also noticed, 'Three men cannot act in concert together in India for five minutes. Each one struggles for power, and in the long run the whole organisation comes to grief.'

Reports of the growing influence of Oriental philosophy in America and the publication of Max Müller's *Ramakrishna: His life and Sayings* by Longmans of London were also filtering in, and since December 1898 itself Swamiji was keenly contemplating visiting the two western continents to have a first hand experience of the growth of the movement, the seeds of which had been planted by him during his first visit in 1893. But his infrequent health prevented him from travelling by sea and he had to shelve his plans. In February 1899 he once again chalked out a plan of giving a four day trial run to test his health by travelling via ship to Madras, and if the journey agreed with him, he would proceed to England from there itself. However, he had to abandon this plan too as it was interfering with his treatment.

Swamiji's health was once again bad in the summer of 1899, and his doctors advised him to desist from giving public lectures. However, he was busy teaching his disciples and holding discourses with the visitors throughout the days, and in the evenings he would sit on the roof of the *bajra*, which is a sort of a houseboat and which had been placed at his disposal by his admirers — the *zemindars* or landlords, of Narail — and he would plunge into deep thought in the twilight stillness of the setting sun. He was also the central figure at the Sunday meetings of the Ramakrishna Mission, and attended both the 26th February lecture on *The Young India Movement* and the 22nd April one on *The Plague and the Duties of the Students*. He also attended several dinner parties given in his honour by the nobility and the gentry of Calcutta.

Swamiji's American disciple, Swami Abhayananda, reached India in February 1899 and on Swamiji's instructions, gave lectures at both Bombay and Madras before reaching Calcutta on 17th March to participate in the birthday celebrations of Sri Ramakrishna, which was held at the Belur Math for the first time. She was given fitting welcomes at both the cities and reciprocated by saying, 'Brothers and Sisters of India. I bring with me the greetings of the people of Chicago in particular and of America in general.' Indeed, the *kaalchakra* or the wheel of time, had moved full circle!

Swamiji had a continuous neuralgic pain all over his chest, and the left side of his chest has been aching since the time he fell ill after the Amarnath *yatra*. His physician, Mahananda *kaviraj* advised him to undertake a sea voyage on a slow moving cargo vessel. However, he had to wait for Swamis Saradananda and Turiyananda to return from Kathiawar — where they had gone to preach — as he wanted to leave the reins of the *Math* with the former, and take the latter with him to the West. On their return to Calcutta on 3rd May, the final plans were set afoot and by this time, it was also decided that Sister Nivedita will also be travelling with them to England. Thus, three tickets were purchased on *S.S. Golconda*, which was to set sail on 20th June.

A farewell meeting was held at *Belur Math* on the 19th night, where members of the monastery presented goodbye addresses to both Swamiji and Swami Turiyananda. Swami Turiyandanda gave a fitting reply, and Swamiji spoke on *Sanyas: Its Ideal and Practice*, in which he stressed on the life of a *sanyasi* as a sacrifice for the welfare of the world. In the afternoon of the 20th the Holy Mother Sarada gave a feast at her Calcutta residence for the two Swamis and all her *sanyasi* children. After that, the two Swamis and Sister Nivedita, accompanied by other *sanyasis*, friends and well-wishers, left for the Princep Ghat from where the ship was to leave around 5 pm. Swamiji was in good spirits and urged all present to be of good cheer, but when the time came for the steamer to leave the jetty, the gathering was in tears, and all of them simultaneously prostrated on the *ghat* in farewell salutation to Swamiji. As long as the ship was in sight, the monks and the devotees kept waving their hands or handkerchiefs.

The *S.S. Golconda* took two days just to steer clear of the hazardous shoals of Diamond Harbour on the Hooghly river, whose navigability has been in jeopardy due to constant silting of its bed since early 16th century. A further two days' sailing across the rough seas of the Bay of Bengal finally found it anchoring at Madras on the night of 24th June 1899.

However, the port of Calcutta had been declared 'plague inflicted', and all vessels arriving from Calcutta were quarantined and no 'native' passenger was allowed to alight at the Madras port. This turned out to be a great disappointment for Swamiji's disciples, friends and admirers at Madras who crowded the pier from early next morning, many of whom even ventured on boats to have a glimpse of Swamiji on the anchored vessel. Basketfuls of mangoes, plantains, coconuts, sweets and local delicacies were sent on board, and Alasinga, not finding an opportunity to consult the Swami, decided to travel with him till Colombo, the next port of calling. The crowd stayed put at the harbour till the *Golconda* sailed out in the evening, amidst a rousing farewell by the waiting multitude.

From Madras, the ship 'rolled and pitched' through the rough seas, and many of the passengers suffered from seasickness. After three days of such rough sailing, the ship docked at Colombo on 28th June. Swamiji's Colombo friends were aware of the Madras episode and had thus procured a prior permit for the landing of Swamiji and his party. At Colombo, Swamiji met, amongst others, the Hindu leaders P. Coomaraswamy and Arunachalam, visited Mrs. Higgins' boarding school for Buddhist girls, and also the monastery and school of the Countess of Canora, an old acquaintance of his. Sister Nivedita was very much impressed with this American born *gerua* saree wearing lady's accomplishment of establishing fifteen schools in Ceylon, including an orphanage and an industrial school. Swamiji was awarded both a grand reception and a grand farewell at Colombo, from where the *Golconda* sailed on the evening of the 28th. Its next stop was Aden. Thus, this voyage of Swamiji was eastward unlike the 1894 journey which had taken him to the West coast of the American continent.

The sea not only remained rough, rather the intensity of the storm grew as the ship advanced, and the monsoon was at its worst near the island of Socotra, some 450 miles east of Aden. The *Golconda* took ten days to cover the normal six-day journey from Colombo to Aden. Again, Aden was out of bounds for the passengers travelling on a ship coming from Calcutta, and Aden being the gateway to Europe, this time the Whites also faced the same fate.

From Aden, the ship travelled on the much calmer Red Sea and halted at Suez for a day to unload some cargo, and then reached Port Said on the Mediterranean end of the Suez Canal; and thereafter, moving through the straits of Messina, it reached Naples in Italy. From there it sailed to Marseilles in France, and then moved on to the Atlantic Ocean through the straits of Gibraltar. After a voyage of forty-two days, the *S.S. Golconda* finally crossed the English Channel and reached London, through the Strait of Dover and into the river Thames off the North Sea, on the morning of 31st July 1899. Mrs. Funke and Christine Greenstidel had come down all the way from the United States to receive Swamiji at London, but Mr. Sturdy was conspicuous by his absence, this in spite of Swamiji having written to him from Port Said. It turned out that Sturdy had also joined the group of deserters like Miss Müller and Mrs. Ashton-Johnson, and although their partings did pain Swamiji, yet he took it in his stride and did not even reply to the rancour shown by Müller and Sturdy.

The sea voyage greatly improved the Swami's health, and it also proved mentally relaxing for him. We gather from Sister Nivedita's account that from the beginning of the voyage till the *Golconda* anchored in London, the 'flow of thought and story went on.' Stories of *Shivaratri*, Prithvi Raj, Vikramaditya, Buddha and Yasodhara, and a thousand more were constantly coming up, 'and a noticeable point was that one never heard the same thing twice.' 'There was the perpetual study of caste, the constant examination and restatement of ideas; the talk of work, of past, present and future, and above all, the vindication of humanity, never weakened, always rising to new heights of defence of the undefended...' Swamiji vehemently protested some European reference to cannibalism by logically putting it thus, 'No nation ever ate human flesh, save as a religious sacrifice, or in war, out of revenge. Don't you see that is not the way of gregarious animals! It would cut at the roots of social life.' On impulse he would say that all religions worship creation, but few have dared to worship death too; the worshippers of Kali do that, they worship the terrible because it is terrible. 'The heart must become a burial ground; pride, selfishness, and desire all broken into dust. Then, and then alone will the Mother dance there.'

Swamiji would lament that while 'self' renders all calculations wrong, it is also the main motivating factor for people to seek God. He would speak about the greatness of Sri Ramakrishna, his associations with various disciples, and also about other saints like Pawhari Baba, Trailanga Swami, and Raghunath Dass. (Dass was an erstwhile soldier in the British service, who could not resist the call of the 'Ram Ram' chantings and joined the chanting party giving wind to his duties, knowing fully well that the penalty for it was to be shot to death. He was saved by Lord Ram himself from being found out by the Colonel who had come to verify reports of his trysts). Swamiji would say that a *sanyasi* takes two vows, one to realise the truth and the other to help the world, and added, that it was also necessary for the *sanyasi* to 'renounce any thought of heaven.'

Swamiji would also deal with the history of the places that the ship sailed by or docked at, and the patriot that he was, he did not miss a chance to elaborate on the importance of India in the world civilisation. He observed,

'Up till a century ago the whole of the world's demand for cotton clothes, cotton, jute, indigo, lac, rice, diamonds and pearls etc. used to be supplied from India. Moreover, no other country could produce such excellent silk and woollen fabrics ... Again, India has been the land of various spices such as cloves,

San Francisco, California, 1900.

cardamom, peppers, nutmeg and mace. Naturally, therefore, from ancient times, whatever country became civilised at any particular epoch depended upon India for those commodities. This trade used to follow two main routes — one was through land, via Afghanistan and Persia, and the other was by sea — through the Red Sea. The Portuguese, in the meantime, discovered a new route to India, doubling Africa. The fortune of India smiled on Portugal … then came the turn of the French, the Dutch, the Danes, and the English; it is therefore that they are the foremost of all nations now … This the Europeans are unwilling to admit. That India, the India of natives is the chief means and resources of their wealth and civilisation is a fact that they refuse to admit or even understand. We too on our part, must not cease to bring it home to them.

Talking about the Suez Canal, and the ports around it, he observed that,

The Suez Canal is also a thing of remote antiquity. During the reign of the Pharaohs in Egypt, a number of lagoons were connected with one another by a channel and formed a canal touching both seas. During the rule of the Roman Empire over Egypt also, attempts were made to keep the channel open. Then the Mohammedan general Amru, after his conquest of Egypt, dug out the sand and changed certain features of it. After that nobody paid much attention to it till the present canal was excavated by the Viceroy of the Sultan of Turkey under advice and capital from the French.

About Aden he informed that,

The English purchased Aden and built the present town more as a port where their ships could get easy access to coal needed to travel further from the English coast and to offset the French control of the Suez Canal. For the same reasons, other European powers have also made bases along the Red Sea by friendly overtures, purchase or force. The Mediterranean marks the end of Asia, Africa and of ancient civilisations, and the beginning of modern civilisations of the European countries.

On this trip, Swamiji was in England for only about a fortnight during which time he visited few friends and fewer places. Since it was the holiday season, the Swami was also not involved in any public work. However, an intimate contact was established with all the members of the Nobel family of Wimbledon, where the Swami had put up at the Limes lodge. Nivedita's younger sister May, her brother Richmond, and her mother Mrs. Samuel Richmond Nobel were all enamoured by the Swami's charismatic personality and holiness.

Mrs. Funke and Christine Greenstidel were already there in London to take the Swami to the United States, and now invitations were pouring in

The S.S. *Numidian* docked at New York on the morning of 28th August 1899, and Swamiji once again set foot on the American soil after almost three and a half years. The holiday season was on in New York too, and Swamiji took the opportunity to recuperate. He stayed at the country home of his old friends Mrs. and Mr. Francis Leggett of Ridgley, in the Hudson River valley, some ninety miles away from New York and near the beautiful Catskill Mountains.

The Leggetts' household at Ridgley was a large one, and Swamiji had many visitors coming there to meet him during his ten-weeks' stay there. He was especially elated to see his brother-disciple

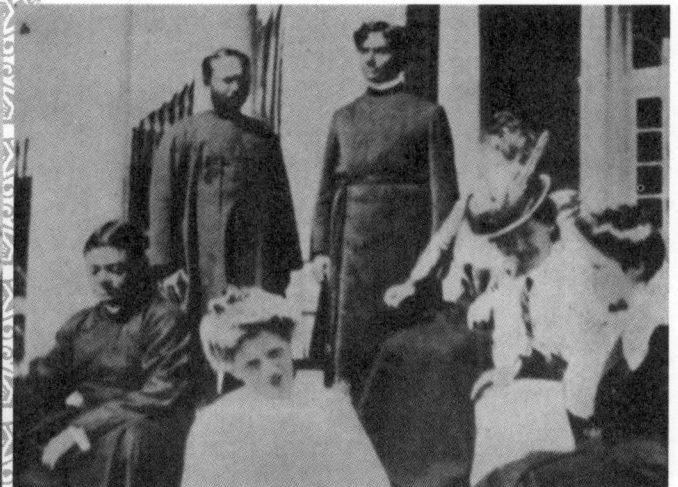

every day from America. So Swamiji decided to travel to that country, and accompanied by Swami Turiyananda and the two American disciples, he took a train to Glasgow — situated on the tidal limits of the river Clyde which opens into the North Channel in the Atlantic Ocean — from where they boarded the S.S. *Numidian* that set sail for America on 17th August 1899. The sea was smooth and beautiful, for the nights were moonlit. The days passed by in the reading and exposition of the *Gita*, in reciting and translating Sanskrit poems and stories and chanting *Vedic* hymns.

Swami Abhedanand, whom he had last met in London in December 1896. Sister Nivedita also arrived from London on 20th September, and Mrs. Ole Bull and her daughter Olea on 7th October. While these two ladies stayed on till Swamiji left Ridgley in early November, the McKinley sisters —

The Ridgely Manor, 1899 ; Sitting (left to right): Swami Vivekananda, Alberta Sturges, Mrs. Francis Leggett (partly hidden), Miss Josephine MacLeod, An unidentified friend; Standing (left to right): Swamis Turiyananda and Abhedananda.

(opp.): In a picnic party at Pasadena, 1900.

Isabelle and Harriet — from Chicago, Miss Ellen Waldo from New York, Mrs. Florence M. Adams from Chicago, and Dr. Egbert Guernsey's daughter Florence from New York came on shorter visits. Then there was the famous New York osteopath Dr. Helmer who was called in by the Leggetts to diagnose Swamiji's illness and to treat him. The doctor did not find anything serious and only advised proper diet.

At Ridgley, Swamiji kept himself busy by writing a book entitled *India and Her People,* learning French, trying his hand at golf, walking in the countryside, and learning to draw from Maud Stumm. Cared for by loving friends, he rested in this country retreat and was a source of joy and inspiration for his hosts, their family, and their other guests.

Swamiji arrived in New York on 7th November and presided over the meeting of the *Vedanta Society* at its new address in New York. Swami Abhedanand, who had been conducting the work of the Society with great success since his arrival in America in August 1897, introduced Swamiji to the members gathered there. Swamiji then devoted the evening to questions and answers. Swamiji was delighted with the progress that the society had made in his absence. A public reception was given to Swamiji on 10th October in the Library of the Society, where many of his old friends and disciples came to meet their beloved teacher and were overjoyed to have him once again amongst them. A large number of men and women, who had come to know about him through his books — that had first been published in 1896 — now came to meet him personally.

During the short period Swamiji stayed in New York, there was great rejoicing at the Vedanta Home. Swamiji did not give any public lectures, but he attended the classes and meetings at the Vedanta Home, and there he gave short talks and answered questions. The inclement New York weather and the emotional shock of the sudden encounter with Swami Kripananda — who had betrayed him earlier — and the almost simultaneous receipt of a bitter letter of dissension from Sturdy, took its toll on the Swami's sensitive body, which he himself described as 'this sort of nervous body is just the instrument to play great music at times and at times to moan in darkness.'

Swamiji thus had to leave New York only after a fortnight's stay. On 22nd November, he left for Chicago where he spent a week, and then moved on to California. In Chicago, he put up with the Hale family at 52 Walton Place and met many of his old friends and disciples, as well as many people who were attracted to his teachings by just reading his books.

The Swami arrived in Los Angeles in the early afternoon of 3rd December where he was to be the guest of Mrs. S. K. Blodgett, an acquaintance of Miss McLeod and an attendee at the Parliament of Religions in Chicago six years earlier. Before this, however, the Swami and Miss McLeod had put up for a week at the home of a Miss Spencer, who later became one of his ardent disciples. Although the Swami came unannounced to the city, he soon found himself surrounded by people who had read his books and were anxious to see and hear him. One such gentleman was Bernhard R. Baumgartner, secretary of the Southern California Academy of Sciences and a versatile man of many talents and accomplishments. He became greatly interested in the Swami's work and even rented the Blanchard Hall, the best in the city, to hold Swamiji's lecture on *The Vedanta Philosophy, or Hinduism as a Religion* on 8th December. Swamiji enthralled the more than six hundred people who attended the lecture, amongst whom were the Mead sisters of South Pasadena — Carrie Mead Wyckoff, Alice Mead Hansbrough, and Helen Mead — all three of whom went on to play important roles in the service of Swamiji's work on the West Coast. The second lecture *The Cosmos or the Vedic Conception of the Universe* was delivered on 12th December at a

In California, 1900.

bigger venue, the Unity Church, which was attended by over a thousand people. This lecture was also a grand success, and there was demand for more. Swamiji, now recovered and charged fully, was also eager to spread his mission to new horizons. The Mead sisters started arranging classes for Swamiji at different places, which continued at the Home of Truth till the very last day of that year. The combination in Swami Vivekananda of 'the learning of a university president, the dignity of an archbishop, with the grace and winsomeness of a free and natural child' won him many admirers and followers, but his ultra radical teachings ruffled some Christian missionaries and "teachers of metaphysics and many pseudo-teachers who resented him or maliciously condemned him either because he was so far superior to them or because he exposed their shallowness and 'spoiled their business' by teaching true metaphysics."

Swami Vivekananda was sought after not only as a great religious teacher, but also as one with an exceptional personality. He could enliven any

At the house of Mrs. Wycoff at Pasadena 1900.

gathering and brighten up any household. In the New Year, he shifted his lectures to the more secular Payer's Hall, where his Sunday the 7th January lecture on *Christ's Message to the World* drew a large overflowing crowd and brought out his 'profound reverence for the highest Christian ideal as embodied in and empowered by Christ.'

In January 1900 itself the Swami accepted the hospitality of the three Mead sisters and shifted to their residence in the nearby town of South Pasadena, where he stayed till mid February and gave lectures almost every day. Although his first lecture was on 15th January at the famous Green Hotel, yet the largest number of his lectures in Pasadena were held at the Shakespeare Club, one of the most prominent women's clubs of southern California. At Pasadena, his lectures covered religious topics, India, his Mission, and even art. Aside from lecturing, he also held small outdoor classes for interested students, and on those rare days when he did not have a class, the child in him would once again manifest and he would play in the Meads' back garden with Mrs. Wyckoff's seventeen-year-old son Ralph and Mrs. Hansbrough's four-year-old daughter Dorothy.

In all his lectures and classes of this period, Swamiji stressed on practical *Vedanta* and yoga as the means of gaining complete control over one's mind and being free. Long ago, Sri Ramakrishna had described the Swami as an unsheathed sword, and in spite of the passage of time, this remained true. He preached a 'man-making' religion and would come down on unjust and ill-informed critics of Indian institutions and traditions. This habit of his earned him many enemies who took recourse to scandal mongering, but that did not perturb Swamiji in any way. His last recorded lecture in Pasadena was on *The Great Teachers of the World* which he delivered on 3rd February. It was during this period only that the *Vedanta Societies* of Los Angeles and Pasadena came into being. Swamiji hoped that such Societies would start a two-way flow of aid between India and America; spiritual help would flow from the East to the West, and financial help the other way round.

Swamiji found the Pacific coast receptive to *Vedantic* ideals, and his health having improved, he decided to extend his work in Los Angeles. At around this time itself, the Swami received an invitation from Reverend Benjamin Fay Mills — an acquaintance from the Chicago Parliament of Religions — to speak at the Congress of Religions to be held in February at Oakland, across San Francisco. Mrs. Hansbrough reached San Francisco before Swamiji and made arrangements for his lectures, prior to his speech at the Congress. Swamiji reached San Francisco on 22nd February and delivered his first lecture there on the 23rd. However, his presence came to be widely known only after his lecture at the Congress of Religions on Sunday, the 25th of February; the lectures at the Congress being spread across eight Sundays in January and February of 1900, with each of the eight invited speakers delving in the viewpoints of different religions on different days. The lectures were all well attended, with Swamiji's *The Claims of Hinduism on the Modern World* being the maximum crowd puller and leading to a second lecture, which took place after the Congress was over, on *Vedanta and Christianity* on 28th February. Swamiji was so much in demand after these two lectures that he had to deliver two series of paid lectures in Oakland in March itself. Swamiji's first lecture *The Laws of Life and Death*, in which he had remarked, 'Not how to go to heaven, but how one can stop going to heaven — this is the object of the search of the Hindu', was totally a new concept and, as the papers said the following day, 'Swami Vivekananda … has set Oaklanders thinking'. In his other lectures, the Swami presented a true picture of India's culture and ideals, uprooting from his listeners' minds the old distorted images and attitudes that probably blocked the reception of his country's great spiritual gifts.

All along this time Swamiji was rooted in San Francisco, from where he would take the ferry service to go to Oakland for his lectures. He continued working steadily and successfully with the active support and help of Mrs. Hansbrough and one Mrs. Benjamin Aspinall. All over the West, Swamiji had 'hands and hearts ready to help him', and Swamiji once commented about this to Mrs. Hansbrough, 'The Mother dropped me in a strange world, among a strange people who do not understand me and whom I do not understand. But the longer I stay here, I have come to feel that some of the people in the West whom I have met belong to me, and they also are here to serve the work assigned to me.'

Swami Vivekananda stayed in San Francisco till the second week of April, during which time he gave several lectures on various topics and held daily classes at his 1719 Turk Street flat. He also held evening lectures thrice a week in the Washington Hall of the Red Men's Building in downtown San Francisco, and Sunday afternoon lectures at the centrally located Union Square Hall. His lectures at San Francisco covered *Gyana Yoga*, *Raja Yoga*, *Vedanta* and *Bhakti Yoga*, and brought him many a follower. One such follower, Thomas Allan's experience of listening to Swamiji convinced him that he had heard 'not a man, but a god.' Each of his lectures were powerful and would bring out his superiority and mastery of the subject to his listeners, but almost invariably, after each such lecture, he would go with a small group of his followers to some nearby restaurant for supper or an ice-cream, and once again become the approachable, loving and unfailing friend.

Swamiji's health continued to improve in California, where he took time to travel on outings on San Francisco's cable cars, which criss-crossed through virtually every nook and corner of the city. Here Swamiji was at complete peace with himself, which was brought out in the 28th March letter that he wrote to Sister Nivedita from San Francisco, in which he penned thus, 'The seed must die underground to come up as the tree. The last two years were the underground rotting. I never had a struggle in the jaws of death, but it meant a tremendous upheaval of the whole life. One such brought me to Ramakrishna, another sent me to the U.S., this has been the greatest of all. It is gone — I am so calm that it astonishes me sometimes.'

After having founded a formal *Vedanta Society* in San Francisco on 14th April, Swamiji moved on to Alameda, a small town near Oakland, where he had lectured several times earlier. One of these, entitled *Mind — Its Power and Possibilities* was presented before a group of women whose purpose was 'to study the art of living and to apply it to the service of humanity.' This time he started off with a series of lectures on *Raja Yoga*, the science of 'how to control the mind so that it is not thrown out of balance, into wave-forms.' During his leisure hours he would often speak informally to intimate groups of students, sometimes entertaining them with stories and jokes. But there was always the undertone of a serious state of mind, and his 'glowing words on spiritual matters … would afford lasting peace to a troubled heart.' In Alameda, Swamiji was in a high state of spirituality and strived to break all bonds for that ecstasy which he had experienced in Dakshineswar in the past. He would hear his Master's voice calling him and feel 'the same infinite ocean of peace, without a ripple, a breath …. Behind my work was ambition, behind my love was personality, behind my purity was fear, behind my guidance the thirst for power! Now they are vanishing and I drift.'

Swami Vivekananda had delivered around a hundred lectures during his four and a half months' work on the Pacific coast. A young woman, Ida Ansell — who attended a large number of the Swami's lectures on both sides of the San Francisco Bay — had taken shorthand notes of these lectures, which were later incorporated in *The Complete Works of Swami Vivekananda* brought out in 1963.

Swamiji had exerted himself too much in California as a result of which his improving health took a beating, and by the end of April, he was physically exhausted. He was contemplating taking some rest and availed of an invitation to spend some time at a small private camp in the Camp Taylor area north of San Francisco, where he spent two weeks resting. He returned to San Francisco in the middle of May, but was still too weak to resume his lectures. He was therefore confined within the residence of his disciple Dr. Milburn H. Logan, where another physician, Dr. William Forster also attended him. It was only on 24th May that he could deliver his first address after the recess, and this time he spoke on the *Bhagvad Gita*, which was the subject matter also of his next three lectures.

Francis Leggett.

(opp.): In a cable car at Mt. Lowe Pasadena, January, 1900.

Towards the end of May, Swamiji received a pressing invitation from Mr. and Mrs. Leggett in London to join them in Paris in July. Swamiji also received an invitation to attend the Congress of the History of Religions to be held in September as part of the Paris Exposition of 1900. Swamiji accepted these invitations but decided to spend a few weeks in New York before sailing for Europe. He therefore left California on 29th May for the East Coast and stopped at Chicago for four days. Swamiji arrived in New York on 7th June, and put up at the *Vedanta Society* there, which had by then shifted to a four-storey building at 102 East Fifty-eighth Street.

Swamiji was extremely pleased with the advancement of the Society under the able leadership of Swami Abhedananda. Swami Turyiananda and Sister Nivedita were also present in New York then. Many of the city's elite were either honorary members of the Society itself or were sympathetic to the Swami's work. However, the hot

summer month of June had many of the citizens fleeing to the mountains or the sea, and Swamiji restricted his work in New York to just four Sunday lectures, and an identical number of classes on the *Gita* on Saturday mornings. Swamiji's old friends took full advantage of the holiday season to 'bask in the sunshine of his presence'.

While Sister Nivedita sailed for France on 28th June, Swamiji, accompanied by Swami Turyiananda left New York for Detroit on 3rd July. One Miss Minnie C. Bock, a member of the New York *Vedanta Society* and a student of Swami Abhedananda who had earlier donated a 160 acres plot in San Antonio Valley in Santa Clara County, California, also accompanied Swami Turyiananda, who later proceeded to California from Detroit to lead the *Vedanta* movement there and to establish the *Shanti Ashram*, or 'Peace Retreat', at the donated plot. At Detroit, Swamiji stayed with the Greenstidel family and mainly rested there, returning to New York on 10th July to rest and oversee the publication of some of his books before sailing for Europe.

It was also at this time that Swamiji took the help of his New York disciple Henry Van Hagen to design the logo of the Ramakrishna Order, about which the Swami explained thus, "The wavy waters are symbolic of Karma; and lotus of Bhakti; and the rising sun of Gyan. The encircling serpent is indicative of Yoga and the awakened Kundalini Shakti, while the swan in the picture stands for Parmatman (Supreme Self). Therefore the idea is that by the union of Karma, Gyan, Bhakti and Yoga, the vision of the Parmatman is obtained."

Swamiji left the shores of the US on 26th July 1900. Here he had spent a total of about thirty-nine months in the two trips that he had made — during which period he had spread his message from one end of the country to the other, established *Vedanta*

societies on both coasts, and had deputed able brother-disciples to carry on the work.

The *S.S. Champagne* reached Le Havre on the noon of 3rd August, and the very same day, Swamiji took the train to Paris. Initially, he was the guest of Gerald Nobel, an old family friend of the Leggetts, and thereafter of the Leggetts themselves. However, in order to master the French language before his speech at the Congress, Swamiji soon moved in with Monsieur Jules Bois, a well-known writer and a student of comparative religion, who spoke only French.

While with the Leggets, Swamiji met many distinguished people from all walks of life, and exchanged ideas with leading thinkers of the West. He would also frequently meet Acharya Jagdish Chandra Bose, the famous botanist, who had been invited to the Paris Exposition in connection with the Congress of Scientists. The keen observer that he was, Swamiji took the opportunity of his presence at the Paris Exposition to study the intricacies of French culture, much of which he penned down in an article entitled *The East and the West*.

The Congress of the History of Religions, a part of the Paris Exposition itself, was a six-day affair, which commenced on 3rd September at the Sorbonne. The Congress dealt exclusively with scholarly matters relating to the historical evolution of the different established religions and no discussions of any doctrine or belief was allowed. Due to his not being in good health at the time, the Swami could speak only twice at the Congress, of which one was an extempore discourse on the origin of the *Shalagram Shila* and the *Shivalinga*, necessitated to counter the allegation of the German Orientalist Gustav Oppert that the origin of the two lay in mere phallicism. Swamiji adduced

proof from the *Atharva Veda Samhita* and other *Vedas* to trace the origin of the *Shivalinga* in the *Yupa Stambha*, or *Skambha*, the sacrificial post idealised in Vedic ritual as the symbol of the Eternal Brahma. Later on, the combined effect of the Vedic ritual, involving the *yagya* fire, its smoke, ashes and flames etc., led to the visualisation of the brightness of Shiva's body in the *Yupa Stambha*, and with time, it came to be worshipped as the *Shivalinga*. In tracing the evolution of the *Shalagram Shila*, Swamiji referred to the influence of Buddhism on the Hindus, who adopted the custom of erecting *stupas*, resembling their *Skambha*, as memorials. The *Shalagram Shilas* are natural stones resembling the artificially cut *Dhatu Garbha*, the stone receptacles for the relics that were deposited in the Buddhist *stupas*. It was the *Vaishnavites* who started the worship of the *Shalagram Shilas*. Swamiji strongly proclaimed that although after the downfall of Buddhism in India, a degenerate period had brought on the association of sex with *Shivalinga*,

Sister Nivedita

yet associating either of the two with sex now is tantamount to associating the practice of the Holy Communion in Christianity with cannibalism.

The other time he spoke at the Congress was to deliver his scheduled speech on the morning of 7th September. In this discourse, he dwelt on the historic evolution of the religious ideas in India. He said that the *Vedas* are not the source of Hinduism only, but also of Buddhism, Jainism and other forms of religious beliefs emanating in India. He also contended that the *Gita* had to be either a prelude to, or contemporaneous with the *Mahabharat*, the thought and the language of both being the same, and the descriptions incorporated in both, contemporary. Swamiji reproved the biasness and the shallowness of the western scholars in their Indian research, and urged them to try and discover the hidden truths instead of writing fanciful articles. In disproving the western contention of primarily Greek influence over everything Indian, he argued that, historically, unless one Hindu who had known Greek could be brought forward, one ought not even talk about Greek influence over Indian science or culture.

In Paris also Swamiji was continuously contemplating on the advancement of the mission entrusted to him by Sri Ramakrishna, and was preoccupied with the yet unregistered trust deed of the *Math* at Belur. He finally got it duly executed at the British Consulate in Paris in August 1900. He also engaged himself in completing the training of Sister Nivedita, who had accompanied him to Paris, so that she could become truly 'dedicated to the Mother's work'. Although she had chosen to be the disciple of Swami Vivekananda of her own free will, yet she was still not able to concentrate in the service of the cause she had received from her Master with all her devotion and loyalty, and extraneous ideas still fascinated her and drew the loyalty of her heart.

After the Congress, Swamiji and Jules Bois accepted an invitation of Ole Bull and became her guests at the house she had taken at Perros-Guirec, a small village on the English Channel. Swamiji stayed there for a fortnight starting from 17th September, and during this time he spoke mostly about Lord Buddha and his teachings, and

In San Francisco, 1900.

highlighted the differences and similarities of ideas of the *Adwaita* and Buddhist school of thoughts. Sister Nivedita was also at Mrs. Bull's place at that time, but she left for England even before her Master had left for Paris; and it would be more than a year and a half before she would meet him again.

Swami Vivekananda returned to Paris in the last week of September and was once again in the most distinguished company. He would never miss an opportunity to point out the influence of India over the thought process of the entire humanity. He found in the Europeans an ad-mixture of Asian and semi-Asian races, intermingled with German, Gaulish and Spanish barbarians, and also found the influence of medieval Arabia on its culture. His encyclopaedic knowledge would hold many numb and few had much to counter his authentic statements.

In Paris, Swamiji became intimate with a former Carmelite monk and Catholic priest, Pere Hyacinthe, who resigned from his monastic order after he fell out with the Church on the doctrine of papal infallibility as pronounced at the First Vatican Council in 1870, and was promptly excommunicated. Thereafter he came to be known as Monsieur Charles Loysun, but he continued to advocate certain reforms in the Church, similarities of which were taken up a century later at the Second Vatican Council held in 1962-63. When Swamiji met him in August 1900, this ageing priest, loved and admired by some, hated and censured by others, was nevertheless very much renowned. Swamiji became very fond of him and had long discussions with him on religious matters, spiritual life, and sects and creeds.

Among the other notable acquaintances that Swamiji developed in Paris were Professor Patrick Geddes, the young Duke of Richelieu; Sir Hiram Maxim of the machine-gun fame; Madame Sarah Bernhardt, the celebrated actress and Madame Calve, the celebrated opera singer, the last three of whom he had known earlier. Swamiji's western

disciple Miss Josephine McLeod, who had been to India earlier also, found in the Swami a Master and a friend, and was his constant companion during his days in Paris.

Madame Calve decided not to sing that winter but to take rest in the temperate climate of Egypt and invited Swamiji to accompany her as her guest. Accordingly, Swamiji along with Jules Bois, Josephine McLeod and the Loysons, accompanied her and boarded the transcontinental Orient Express on 24th October for Constantinople. Their first stopover was Vienna where they stayed for three days from 25th October onwards. They visited many places of interest, including the Schonberg Palace where Napoleon's son was interned and eventually

Emma Calve.

died of a broken heart, an episode immortalised in a play of Sarah Bernhardt. In fact, the Swami had recently watched her perform the same. Each room of this palace was thematically furnished and decorated with the artefacts of a particular country, including India and China.

Having left Vienna on 28th October, the train passed through Hungary, Serbia, Romania and Bulgaria and reached Constantinople on the 30th. While travelling through Europe, Swamiji found it bristling with portents of war and remarked that 'Europe is a vast military camp', and rightly prophesied, 'After the death of the present Austrian Emperor (Francis Joseph, who died in 1916), Germany will surely try to absorb the German-speaking portion of the Austrian Empire, and Russia and others are sure to oppose her, so there is the possibility of a dreadful war.'

At Constantinople, Swamiji visited the Museum of Antiquities, the foreign quarters, the ancient walls, the fortress of seven towers, and also enjoyed a panoramic view of the historic city of Istanbul, with its many ancient mosques, columns, minarets, towers and domes, from a site across the Golden Horn. He met several distinguished persons of the city and although not allowed to speak from a public platform, held several private conversations and drawing room talks on the religion of *Vedanta*.

Monsieur Pere Hyacinthe was also there in Egypt at that time, and Swamiji decided to visit him at Scutari, across the river Bosporus, where he was staying at the American College of Girls. Accompanied by Miss Mcleod, they hired a boat by communicating in sign language to the Arab or Turkish speaking boatmen, and on their way they also saw a Sufi *fakir* singing. They also had the experience of dining at the famous Scutary Cemetery. It was at Scutary that Swamiji gave his only public lecture on Hinduism at the American College for Girls on 2nd November.

Swamiji and party was there in Constantinople for about ten days, after which they took a steamer for Athens. On their way, they visited the Archipelago islands, off the Sea of Marmara. One of these islands had an Orthodox Greek Monastery that the Swami visited. It was on another such island that Swamiji met the distinguished Professor R.L. Lepper, whom the Swami knew when the latter was a professor at the Pachaiyappa's College, Madras.

The steamer finally reached the Athenian port Piraeus, a small but beautiful town with a European air about it. During the three days' stay at Athens, Swamiji visited the Acropolis, the marble temple of the Wingless Victory, the Parthenon, the temple of Olympian Zeus, Theatre Dionysus, and of course the Elusis, an ancient Greek city and the chief religious seat. On the fourth day, Swamiji and party boarded the Russian steamer *Czar* for Egypt.

Although Swamiji did some sightseeing in Egypt — the famous Cairo Museum, the Sphinx, and the Pyramids — yet, in his heart he seemed to be withdrawn from all external matters. He was tired, homesick, and concerned about his great friend and disciple Captain Sevier who was reportedly on his deathbed since the last week of October. He became restless to return to India. Therefore, he took leave of his companions, Madame Calve who had addressed him as 'Mon Pere' or My Father, Miss McLeod, to whom he was a prophet and a saint, and Jules Bois, who considered him a great thinker and a man of God. And on the night of 26th November 1900, he boarded the Italian steamer *S.S. Rubbatino* which was sailing to Bombay.

When the ship docked at Bombay on 6th December, Swamiji was full of joy at being so close to meeting his disciples. He landed at Bombay totally unannounced and immediately took the Bombay Express bound for Calcutta. In the train, he came across his old friend Manmathanath Bhattacharya, and the three days passed off well for both of them.

It was quite late in the evening of 9th December 1900 and the monks and *bhramacharis* were taking their dinner at the Belur *Math*, when the gardener came running in exclaiming that a *sahib* had come. As the gathering was speculating who the *sahib* could be, and what could have brought him so late in the night, in came Swami Vivekananda to the great excitement of one and all. At once an *asana* was spread out for him to sit, and he was served a large helping of the *khichuri* prepared for dinner that night. It was many months since he had had it, and Swamiji partook of the food with great zest.

There was no sleeping that night as the monks sat through hours of enlightening descriptions by Swamiji of his experiences in the West. He told them that although initially he was impressed with the power, organisation and apparent democracy of the Occident, he later realised that the progressive spirit of the West was composed mostly of greed, selfishness, exploitation, and struggle for power. He was in fact more impressed with China of which he said later sometime, 'I see before me the body of an elephant. There is a foal within. But it is a lion-cub that comes out of it. It will grow in future, and China shall become great and powerful.'

Swami Vivekananda was once again back in his world where he found that 'everything is green and gold, and the grass is like velvet, yet the air is cold and crisp and delightful.' However, in both health and emotion, his heart was in a bad shape. Physically, he was having some problems with his heart, and he had also come to know of the demise of Captain Sevier on 28th October at Mayavati. Swamiji at once sent a telegram to Mrs. Sevier and left Calcutta on 27th December en route Kathgodam to Mayavati.

Accompanied by Swamis Shivananda and Sadananda, Swamiji arrived at Kathgodam on the 29th and was received there by Swami Virajananda, who had come from Mayavati, and Lala Govind Sha, who was sent by Swamiji's Almora friend Lala Badri Sha. After resting for a day at Kathgodam, Swamiji proceeded straight to Mayavati. The inclement weather and snowfall slowed down the progress of the party and it took them almost four-and-a-half days to cover the sixty-five miles climb to Mayavati. As a result, New Year's eve was spent at an unscheduled halt at a small roadside shop.

Swamiji reached Mayavati on 3rd January 1901 and stayed there till the 18th. He was relieved to find Mrs. Sevier to have overcome the shock gracefully. From her he learnt that Captain Sevier had adopted austerity and poverty on principle and had decided not to go out of Mayavati even for the treatment of his deteriorating urinary problem. Rather he had chosen to endure the pain by taking the name of God. He was pleased to learn that Mrs. Sevier was locally known as the 'Mother of Mayavati'. Swamiji was happy at the growth and

for himself he would do all that he could, but he needed assurance of cooperation, and he needed the other brother monks to stay at the Mayavati *Ashram* for at least three years continuously. Swamiji fully agreed with this contention and when everybody gathered around him, broached the subject. While all agreed to commit thus, Swami Virajananda humbly but firmly declared that he

Adwaita Ashrama, at Mayavati.

maintenance of the *Ashram* that had been done by the Seviers. Two important occasions — Swamiji's 38ᵗʰ birthday and Captain Sevier's 56ᵗʰ birthday — fell during his stay at Mayavati.

Much as the Swami desired to have long walks at Mayavati, the snow compelled him to stay mostly indoors. He was in high spirits, but his health let him down and he had several attacks of asthma, which became a cause of concern for all those who were with him. When he was better, Swamiji had intense discussions with Swami Swarupananda about the *Ashram*'s work, and the latter said that as

intended to pass some time in secluded meditation and living off alms, and even Swamiji's advice — 'Don't ruin your health by practising austerities, but try to profit by our experience. We have subjected ourselves to extreme austerities, but what has been the result the break down of our health in the prime of manhood' — could not dissuade him from his resolve, which was later appreciated by Swamiji in his absence.

The one thing of the *Ashram* that Vivekananda did not appreciate was the regular ritualistic worship of the photograph of Sri Ramakrishna, which was installed in the shrine room there. He disapproved of any ritual worship in the *Adwaita Ashrama*, where only subjective religious practices like meditation, studying the scriptures, and teaching of the highest spiritual monism were allowed and no dualistic weakness was to be encouraged in any manner. However, the Swami did not use his power in any way to dismantle the worship-room, and, instead wanted them to see their mistake and rectify it. After Swamiji's death, Swami Vimalananda did try to appease Mother Sarada to approve of a shrine for Sri Ramakrishna at Mayavati, but the Holy Mother also stressed on the *Adwaita*, and ultimately, the shrine itself was abolished on 18th March 1902.

Swamiji left Mayavati on 18th January 1901, and after passing through Champawat and Tanakpur, the party reached Pilibhit on the fourth day. From Pilibhit, Swamiji boarded a train for Calcutta and in the train itself Swamiji came to know the news of the death of his beloved disciple, the Raja of Khetri. He had been in Agra and had fallen off the eighty-six feet high tower of Sikandra. The news came as a great shock to the Swami and he reached Calcutta with a heavy heart on the morning of 24th January.

His reaching the *Belur Math* the same afternoon brought about rejoicing amongst the brother-disciples and other disciples present there, who wished that the Swami's stay this time would be much longer than the eighteen days that he had spent here before leaving for Mayavati. His first formal engagement in Belur was the prize-distribution ceremony of Belur M.E. School where he spoke on the practical educative aspects of learning handicrafts by the students, and also stressed on the importance of health, character and good manners.

Towards the end of January, Miss McLeod was in Calcutta on her way to Japan, and she took the opportunity to call on Swami Vivekananda. Mrs. Sevier was also expected anytime in Calcutta on her way to England. Swamiji had earlier contemplated accompanying Mrs. Sevier to England, but as he wrote to Mrs. Bull, he now wanted to go 'on a long pilgrimage with … mother,' who had wished to go on a pilgrimage to the holy places in East Bengal and Assam. En route his aborted destination of Nepal, Monsieur Jules Bois also came to the *Math* on 17th February.

However, before he left on the pilgrimage with his mother, Swami Vivekananda decided to create a legal authority to manage the *Math*, and executed a trust deed on 30th January 1901. It was registered on 6th February with the Sub-Registrar's Office at Howrah. All the *Belur Math* properties were vested in this Trust and the first trustees were Swamis Brahmananda, Premananda, Shivananda, Saradananda, Akhandananda, Trigunatitananda, Ramakrishnananda, Adwaitananda, Subodhananda, Abhedananda and Turiyananda. The trust deed provided for the Trustees to elect a President from amongst themselves, and the first meeting in this direction was held on Sunday, 10th February, where Swami Brahmananda was elected the first president of the *Math*, with Swamis Saradananda and Nirmalananda as secretary and assistant secretary respectively.

After having celebrated Sri Ramakrishna's sixty-eighth birthday on 24th February at the *Math*, which was attended by more than 30,000 people, Swami Vivekananda, accompanied by a large party of *sanyasis*, left Calcutta for Dacca on 18th March. On reaching Dacca the following afternoon, the Swami was given a grand reception by a large enthusiastic crowd, who took him in a procession to the *zemindar* Mohini Mohan Das's residence, which was put at Swamiji's disposal during his stay at Dacca. He held religious discourses during the next three afternoons, which were attended by several hundreds.

Swamiji's mother, aunt and cousin joined him on 25th March at Narayanganj from where they started their pilgrimage. Their first destination was Langalbandha, connected with the *Puranic* legend of Parashuram. On the occasion of *Buddha-ashtami* more than a hundred thousand people gathered there for the sacred bath in the Brahmaputra River that was 'nearly a mile broad at the place', and wherein Swamiji and party also had a holy dip and performed their *puja*. He next wanted to take his mother to Chandranath, 'a holy place at the easternmost corner of Bengal' near Chittagong. However, before that they returned to Dacca, where Swamiji continued with his afternoon discourses on *gyana, bhakti*, faith, renunciation, discrimination, non-attachment, *Karma Yoga*, etc. He also delivered two well-attended public lectures on 30th and 31st March on *What have I Learnt* and *The Religion We are Born In* respectively.

Swamiji was visiting East Bengal for the first time and he was thrilled with its gurgling rivers, which he called 'rolling oceans of fresh water'. There was greenery all around, clean villages, and people who were hardier and active than their counterparts on the Gangetic plateau. Swamiji also made a short trip from Dacca to Deobhog, Nag Mahasay's village, where he was well cared for by 'that great soul's' wife. Swamiji and party left Dacca on 5th April for Chandranath, from where they proceeded to Kamakhya, the famous shrine of the Divine Mother near Guwahati in Assam. From Guwahati, Swamiji went to Shillong on health grounds. Shillong was then the headquarters of the Government of Assam, the chief commissioner of which was Sir Henry Cotton, a champion of the Indian cause. At the request of Sir Cotton, Swamiji delivered a lecture before the resident English officials and a large gathering of Indians. Sir Cotton also instructed the Civil Surgeon to attend on the ailing Swami, and made daily enquiries about his health. But the long associated diabetes, and the severe attack of asthma that he had had at Dacca, took its toll on Swamiji's health, which was failing rapidly, and sometime in the second week of May he decided to leave for Calcutta.

The party reached Calcutta on 12th May. Swamiji's tour of East Bengal and Assam was virtually his last. His health worsened thereafter and the monks at Belur begged of him to give up all public work and take complete rest. Thus, Swamiji remained in the monastery for the next seven months in complete rest. Everyone around him tried their best to obtain the finest medical treatment for him and to divert his mind to lighter subjects, but the former was easier done than the latter, and the Swami's mind was often in deepest concentration over serious thoughts covering religion, philosophy, sociology and science. Though he was weak of body, his mind was as luminous as ever, and it would have probably been easier to move a mountain than to hold in check the mind that had taught the world. During this time Swamiji also did some casual teaching, and always kept himself abreast of the developments of the work in India, England and America. People also flocked to Belur to take advantage of the Swami's continuous presence and receive his blessings.

It was in December 1901 that the Indian National Congress was holding its session in Calcutta. Swamiji was considered by many of the delegates as the Patriot Saint of Modern India, and many of them took this opportunity to visit the *Belur Math* and pay respects to him. Some began visiting him almost every afternoon. Swamiji enlightened them on various social, political and religious subjects and often these meetings formed a Congress in itself. In the words of one delegate himself, '(these sessions were) of a type even superior and more beneficial to those present than the actual sessions of the Congress'. Among the leaders who visited the *Math* were Mahatma Gandhi, till then still known as M. K. Gandhi, and Bal Gangadhar Tilak. Tilak succeeded in meeting the Swami, but Swamiji was not at the *Math* on the day Gandhiji had come to visit him.

Swamiji in Shillong.

Swami Vivekananda's keen observation of the social dilemma of conversion of the low, the poor and the miserable into Christianity made him comment,

> These are the backbone of the nation, whose labour produces our food. Where is the man in our country who sympathises with them, who shares in their joys and sorrows? Look how, for want of sympathy on the part of Hindus, thousands of pariahs in the Madras Presidency are becoming Christians! Don't think that it is merely the pinch of hunger that drives them to Christianity. It is simply because they do not get your sympathy. Is there any fellow feeling or sense of *Dharma* left in the country? There is only 'Don't-touchism' now! Kick out all such usages.... I see as clear as daylight that the same *Brahma*, the same *Shakti*, that is in me is in them as well. Only, there is a difference in the degree of manifestation that is all. In the whole history of the world, have you ever seen a country rise without a free circulation of the national blood throughout its entire body? If one limb is paralysed, then even with the other limbs whole, not much can be done with that body — know this for certain.

Later on he said, 'After so much *tapasya* I have understood this as the highest truth: God is present in every being. There is no other God besides that. He who serves all beings serves God indeed.'

Vivekananda would move about the *Math* in different *sanyasi* attires and one of his favourite sitting places was on the upper veranda of the monastery building from where one could gaze at the towers of the Dakshineswar temple. Another of his favourite places was under the *bel*, or wood-apple tree by the side of the Ganges, beside which now stands the temple erected in his memory. Yet another of his favourites was under the mango tree in the courtyard located between Sri Ramakrishna's

shrine and the monastery building. His room was in the south-eastern corner of the first floor of the monastery. It was a large room that served both as his living quarters and study, and the same has been preserved by the *Math* in all reverence and with all its furnitures and knick-knacks, most of which were presents from his western disciples. It was in this room that his soul departed from his body, and the calendar on the wall still shows July 4 1902.

Swami Vivekananda had many pets at the *Math*, and he personally tended to them. He milked his goats and fed them every morning, took care of the monastery cows, sheep, ducks, the antelope, and was very fond of his puppy 'Bagha' and a 'beautiful black kid'. Bagha was such a loved pet that, on its death after Swamiji's demise, the monks permitted to inter its body in the *Math* grounds on the banks of the Ganges, and a pile of bricks still mark the burial place. The Swami was always frank and free in his observations, would sing with his brother monks, have fun with them, help them in their difficulties, and lead them on festivities. At the monastery it was all enthusiasm, activity, spiritual fervour and hard training; in short, he was the centre of all activities at the *Math*.

However, Swami Vivekananda's health, far from improving, worsened. In the month of August, he left for Darjeeling for a few days. But the damp weather of Darjeeling proved damaging to his health, and his asthma worsened. He soon returned to Calcutta, but there was no sign of any relief even then. The condition of his health deteriorated with time, and soon he was in a condition of general dropsy, with his feet swollen, making it difficult for him to walk. His body became very sensitive and sleep eluded him, but his spirit was high and he was ever cheerful and ready to receive people. He had surrendered to the will of the Lord, and the *Karma Yogi* only wished to continue working.

Miss McLeod's mission to Japan also included

establishing a centre so that Swami Vivekananda's work could be carried out there. Swamiji had earlier assured her that if the situation demanded, he would personally visit Japan. Okakura, a Japanese friend of Miss McLeod, sent a cheque for Rs. 300 to Swamiji as his passage money. But his precarious health prevented him from venturing on such a long tour.

After taking considerable physical rest during the months of July and August, Swamiji felt somewhat better in September. He observed all the religious festivals that year in the most orthodox manner, so much so that for the Durga Puja he acquired a copy of Raghunandan's *Twenty-eight Tattyas* and performed the *puja* in strict conformity with its injunctions. Sarada *Maa* also attended the *Puja*, which was held in the *Math* on a grand scale and with a *pratima* or an earthen idol, for the first time. This scripture based celebration of the Durga and other *pujas* that were held at the *Math* subsequently also helped in clearing the misunderstandings orthodox Hindus had about the *Math*.

However, Swamiji had fever even during the Durga Puja, and his condition worsened so much after the festivities that Dr. Saunders, a noted physician of Calcutta, had to be called. The doctor advised Swamiji total physical and intellectual rest. This dictum distressed Swamiji who was eager to keep himself busy, and whenever he felt a little better, he would indulge in some or the other manual work, mostly gardening.

His recurring illness reminded his mother Bhuvaneswari Devi of her vow to offer special worship to Mother Kali at Kalighat, and he requested the Swami to come to Kalighat for the occasion. Although Swamiji was still sick, he bowed to his mother's will, and after taking a dip in the *Adi Ganga* flowing past the Kalighat temple, he came to the temple in wet clothes and as desired by his mother, rolled over thrice before the deity and performed prayer, *pradakshin* and *hom* at the temple. Although an *Adwaitin* at heart, Swamiji, like the great Shankaracharya, had fervent devotion to these personal aspects of the Godhead.

The autumn festivities passed by well, but Swami Vivekananda's failing health cast a shadow of gloom over the residents of the *Math*, and to add to their anxiety, his right eye sight had also started to fail. The presence of albumin in his urine, for almost three years then, was telling on his health, and the doctors advised him complete bed rest for the next three months. But, as soon as he was a little well, Swamiji could hardly be made to stay in bed.

From the month of December itself, Swamiji's western disciples started coming to Calcutta to meet their ailing Master. While Mrs. Sevier came back from England on the 9th of the month, Miss Josephine McLeod and her Japanese friends Mr. Okakura and Mr. Hori left Japan on the 7th and reached Calcutta on 6th January 1902. Okakura Kabuzo was the head of the Committee for the Restoration of Old temples and one of the founders of the Tokyo School of Art, and Hori was a zealous Buddhist priest, and the two of them decided to visit India and, amongst other things, to personally invite Swamiji to attend the proposed Congress of Religions to be held in Japan. Vivekananda warmly welcomed the guests and told Okakura, 'We are two brothers who meet again having come from the ends of the earth.' Of Hori, he said, 'He will make an excellent *sanyasi*.' While Hori had come to India to study Sanskrit and English, Okakura came to visit the 'motherland of Japanese culture and art'; but it was also the intention of the latter to seek control of the management of the Mahabodhi Temple at Bodh Gaya and to acquire some land near the temple for building a rest house for the visiting Japanese pilgrims.

Having recovered somewhat, Vivekananda planned to go on a pilgrimage to Varanasi. It was expected that the dry climate of Varanasi would help improve his health. He therefore conceded to Okakura's request to accompany him to Bodh Gaya, on his way to Varanasi. Thus, Swamiji accompanied by Miss McLeod, Mr. Okakura and Swamis Nirbhayananda and Bodhananda left Calcutta on the 27th for his last journey to Bodh Gaya and Varanasi, a fitting end to all his wanderings, as Bodh Gaya had been the first holy place that he had visited at the very beginning of his life as a wandering monk about twelve years ago.

Swamiji was there in Bodh Gaya for about a week, during which time he and his party visited the temple every day, and as was his nature, the Swami explained to the others the history and architecture of all that they saw. While Miss McLeod returned to Calcutta from Gaya, Swamiji and the others proceeded to Varanasi where prior arrangements had been made for Swamiji's stay at the Gopallal Villa in the Ardali Bazar area of the city. As elsewhere, here also Swamiji soon became the centre of attraction for many people, including some of the orthodox pundits. His health improved a little, and he would visit temples and make afternoon trips on the Ganga quite frequently. Here he met Udai Pratap Singh, the Maharaja of Bhinga, at whose insistence and support Swamiji later opened an *Ashram* there. Swamiji was highly appreciative of the work done by the 'Poor Men's Relief Association', which had been formed by several Bengali youths of the city in June 1900 to serve the suffering pilgrims who thronged the city, and which later on came to be known as 'The Ramakrishna Home of Service', and today operates from a bigger place at the Luxa region of the city and is known as 'The Ramakrishna Mission Home of Service'. During his short stay there, the Swami met various people, had discussions with the learned pundits of Varanasi, and initiated some disciples too.

From Varanasi, Swami Vivekananda sent a welcome letter to Mrs. Ole Bull, who had arrived in Calcutta with Sister Nivedita sometime in the first week of February. He wrote 'Welcome to India once more, dear mother (Mrs. Bull) and daughter (Nivedita)...' To Sister Nivedita he wrote, 'If you have to ask my advice or to get anybody to do your business, Brahmananda is the only one I recommend, none else... Do just as the 'Mother' directs... All my powers come unto you — may Mother Herself be your hands and mind. It is immense power, irresistible, that I pray for you, and if possible along with it infinite peace.... If there was any truth in Sri Ramakrishna, may He take you into His leading, even as He did me, nay a thousand times more...' Swamiji had great faith in Sister Nivedita, and had even proclaimed that 'Even if I pass away Nivedita and Shashi (Swami Ramakrishnananda) and others will keep my word. They will do *Thakur*'s (Sri Ramakrishna's) work till the end of their life; they won't waiver in any case. My all hopes rest in them.' In his last letter to her from Varanasi, he had expressed his desire to die 'in this city of Shiva', and directed her on what to do if such a thing really happened. He had ended the letter with the words 'I am quite satisfied with my work; to have left two (Nivedita and Swami Ramakrishnananda) true souls is beyond the ambition of the greatest', and had signed off as 'Ever your loving father.'

In March, Swamiji's health was once again in a bad shape. He had a constant low fever and had difficulty in breathing. Once, he became ill so seriously that, three attendants had to take turns and fan him continuously throughout the night. He therefore took the earliest opportunity to leave for Calcutta, and reached Belur three or four days prior to 11th March, the date on which Sri Ramakrishna's birthday fell that year.

The residents of the *Math* had a glimpse of the power that Swamiji wielded, when one day after his return from Varanasi, his speech on the presence of the omnipresent in all beings magnetised them to such an extent to the peace and insight of deep meditation that Swami Premananda, who was on his way to the shrine after his bath, was rendered motionless for almost fifteen minutes. He could move only after the Swami addressed him, 'Now go for worship'.

The public celebration of Sri Ramakrishna's birthday was on 16th March that year, but the sudden serious turn of Swamiji's health since the past few days had a pall of gloom hanging over the *Math*, and the thousands who had come there, hoping to see and hear him on the occasion, were greatly disappointed. He could not move out of his room and gazed at the gathering for a very short time from the window, supporting himself on its iron bars.

Soon thereafter, Sister Nivedita spoke on 21st March 1902 at the Classic Theatre Hall on *The Hindu Mind in Modern Science*, the grand success of which brought much relief to the Swami. Then on 29th March, work on the embankment of the river was necessitated as the river water entered the *Math* compound at high tide. Work began at the Swami's instance. By the month end Christine Greenstidel arrived in Madras, and in the first week of April, Josephine McLeod left Calcutta for Mayavati, where Sister Nivedita and Christine Greenstidel joined her a month later.

After his return from Varanasi, Swamiji suffered a serious relapse, and at the insistence of the monks, he agreed to be treated by *Kaviraj* Mahanand Sen Gupta, the well-known Ayurvedic practitioner from Calcutta. The treatment was rigorous and Swamiji was not allowed to either drink water or take salt, the two ingredients necessary to live. Swamiji agreed to follow the treatment strictly and for twenty-one days he did not have a single drop of water, such was the control of his mind over his body. After more than two months' treatment, Swamiji felt greatly benefited.

He had great faith in the powers of *brahmacharya*, which he said could help one retain and reproduce exactly what one had heard or read even once, even if it was a long time ago. During his illness, the Swami had read the first ten volumes of the latest edition of the Encyclopaedia Britannica, and he remembered every piece of information in all those ten volumes.

Vivekananda paid little heed to taking complete rest and opposed to setting limits on his teaching also. He did not want earnest seekers to be turned away. He conducted numerous scriptural and question classes till the last day of his life and the *brahmacharis* and monks all came to seek his spiritual advice. He spent much of the day in writing letters, reading, and making notes on Hindu philosophy and Indian history. For recreation he would often sing or have fun with his brother-monks. The Swami was a strict disciplinarian but abhorred extremes. He protested against the elaborate paraphernalia of daily worship in the *Math*, and advised his disciples to devote more time to scriptural study, meditation, and religious discussions. To enforce this, he introduced the periodical ringing of a bell to summon the monks to such activities. He repeatedly pointed out that in order to retain the purity of the Order and the initial vigour for working for social upliftment, it was necessary to have a definite ideal to reach, to maintain the discipline and the vows taken, to perform austerities and meditation, and continue with education and cultural activities.

Swamiji began to feel that his public work has come to an end and that he had been able to initiate the deliverance of the message of his Master to the world. Ignoring his worldwide fame, he lived silently and unostentatiously in the quietness of the *Math* on the bank of the Ganges, sometimes playing the role of a *guru*, or spiritual teacher, sometimes that of a father to his disciples, and sometimes even that of a school master. The visitors found him a personification of humility. He now concentrated all his power and energy into 'man-making', and that too by example. His heart truly wept at the sight of the suffering and degradation of the illiterate Indian masses; his soul glowed with the fire of love for humanity; and his true patriotism

Swamiji in Shillong.

and self-sacrificing zeal did not know what fatigue was; and through all these he showed to his disciples how a God-inspired soul felt and worked for humanity. Through his teachings of the *Vedanta* — which he practised in his life too — Swami Vivekananda proved to his disciples, followers, admirers, friends and the whole world, the ideal of character building through the light and spirit of the *Vedanta*.

In the last two months of his life, Swami Vivekananda engaged himself in activities that proved to be precursors to his death. First, after his return from Varanasi, he wrote to all his *sanyasi* disciples from all around the world to visit him, even if it was for a short time. While some came and could thus meet him for the last time, others who could not come, missed the last opportunity of meeting their leader at whose behest they had dedicated their lives to his cause. Then Swamiji gradually withdrew himself from directing the affairs of the *Math*. He engaged more and more on deep meditations and sought infinite repose. Sri Ramakrishna had said that Naren would merge in *Nirvikalpa Samadhi* the day he realised who he was, and one day the Swami's 'Yes, I know now' reply to one of his brother-monk's query 'Do you know yet who you were, Swamiji?' awed all into a grave silence.

Swamiji's cheerful bearing and his recovering health in June beguiled his purposeful actions from his near and dear ones. Even actions like asking for the Bengali almanac and keeping it with him to search for an auspicious date for some event went unnoticed; so did his stopping Sister Nivedita from coming to the *Math* after her return from Mayavati, and instead, volunteering to visit her at her residence at Baghbazar to examine everything himself and to discuss about her plans; and to bless her, the house and her work. However, at the end of June he declared, 'A great *tapasya* and meditation has come upon me, and I am making ready for death.' He even pointed out the place on the *Math* grounds, on the bank of the Ganges, where he wished to be cremated, and where stands his temple now. On the last *ekadoshi*, just two days before his death, he insisted on serving meal to Sister Nivedita. He even poured water over her hands to wash it, and then dried them with a towel. When Sister Nivedita said, 'It is I who should do these things for you, Swamiji', he answered solemnly, 'Jesus washed the feet of His disciples', and one could virtually comprehend 'it was the last time'.

He had once declared in Kashmir, 'Whenever death approaches me, all weaknesses vanish. I have neither fear, nor doubt, nor thought of the external. I simply busy myself making ready to die.' But there was one attachment that was an exception. 'You know, the work is always my weak point. When I think that might come to an end, I am all undone.'

In the last days of his life, there was nothing sad or grave about the Swami. Rather one could strongly feel the presence of a luminous soul. On the morning of the *Mahasamadhi* itself he rose early and after entering the chapel of the monastery, he closed all its doors and windows. There he must have been in the presence of his Master and the Divine Mother, the two being uniform to him, as hinted by his singing of a beautiful song on Mother Kali at the end of the meditation. Thereafter, he again sat in solitary meditation for three long hours. Unlike his recent routine, he even had his noon meal with his brother monks and disciples. He also expressed three wishes that day; to have the Kali *Puja* performed at the *Math* the next day which was an *amavasya* and a Saturday and thus an auspicious day for performing the same; to do something for Japan, and to meet R.C. Dutta. Later, he asked Swami Shudhananda to read the passage on *Sushumnah Suryashmi* from the *Shukla Yajur Veda*, but was not happy with the interpretation given by the particular author and asked his disciples to discover the true meaning of the passage. In the afternoon, he held a three-hour long class on Sanskrit grammar for the *brahmacharis*, after which he went on a long walk up to the Belur market with Swami Premananda. They discussed, among other things, Swamiji's proposal to found a *Vedic College* to 'kill out superstitions'. After returning to the *Math*, he again talked for a while. Incidentally, this was his last conversation with the monks.

On that Friday, that is 4th July 1902 — a day coinciding with the independence of the country that had given him great fame throughout the world — as evening set in, Swamiji gradually withdrew himself, and when the bell for the evening service rang, he retired to his own room. There he sat in meditation facing the Ganga. He had instructed the monks not to come inside the room unless called for. At around 8 pm he called one of them and requested him to fan his head as he lay quietly on his bed. After about an hour, his hands trembled a little and he took a deep breath. Then all was quiet for about two minutes, whereupon the Swami again took a deep breath and his eyes became fixed in the centre of his eyebrows and there appeared a divine expression on his face indicating that it was all over. It was 9:10 pm then. Swamis Premananda and Nischayananda tried to bring back consciousness by chanting the Master's name. When there was no response even then, Swami Adwaitananda asked Swami Bodhananda to feel Swamiji's pulse; not finding it, the latter cried aloud. Swami Adwaitananda then asked Swami Nirbhayananda to fetch Dr. Mahendra Nath Mazumdar from Baranagar, while another Swami left for Calcutta to inform Swamis Brahmananda and Saradananda who had gone there that day.

The doctor arrived at around 10:30 pm, and even tried to bring him back by artificial respiration, but eventually, pronounced him dead at midnight. He thought it was due to heart failure, while Dr. Bipin Bihari Ghosh of Calcutta, who came the next morning, thought it was due to apoplexy, both contentions being negated by the other doctors who came and heard of the symptoms. The monks however knew that the Swami had voluntarily left his body in a *Mahasamadhi*. Sister Nivedita came in the morning and, sitting by the body of her Master, she continuously fanned his mortal remains till 2 pm when it was taken down to the porch where the *aarti* was performed before taking it for cremation at the spot that the Swami himself had earmarked.

Sadness reigned all over, and grief hung over the monks who had not known such bereavement since the passing away of the Master himself, who had at least given them to Naren's charge; but this time they felt as if they were truly orphaned.

After the earthly remains of the Swami were brought down to the porch, it was placed on a cot,

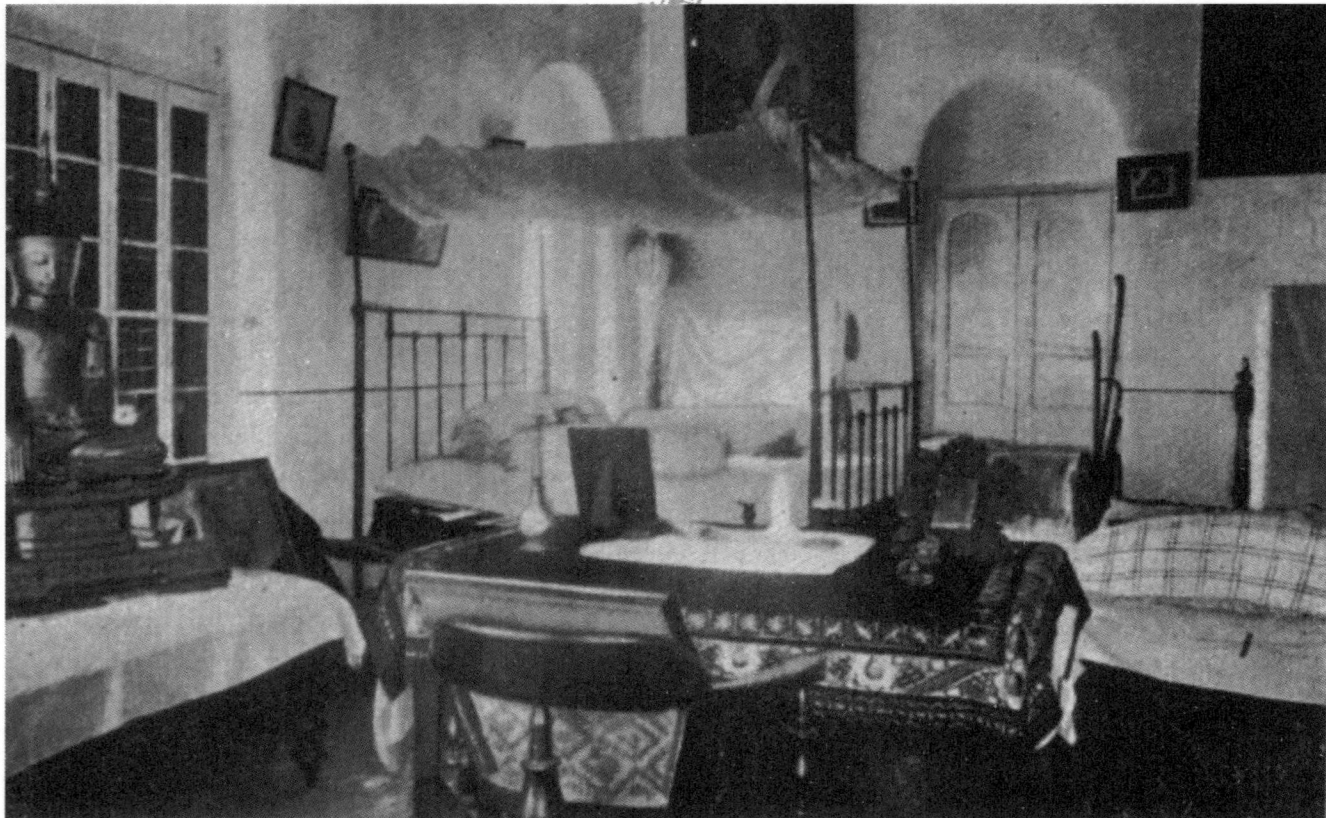

Swami Vivekananda passed away at the age of thirty-nine years, five months and twenty-two days, thus fulfilling a prophecy that he often repeated, 'I shall never live to see forty.' The monks were dumb struck and there was a pall of gloom over the *Math*. Telegraphic messages were sent to all centres across India and abroad. People started pouring in by ferry and road to pay their last respects to the Swami, whose motionless body lay in the room that only a day or two ago had reverberated with his sermons and laughter.

where it lay wrapped in the ochre robes of the *sanyasi*. The *aarti* was carried out with the waving of lamps, reciting of *mantras*, ringing of bells, blowing of conches and burning of incense. For the last time the disciples touched the feet of their Master with their heads. Others fell prostrate on the ground. Then the body — amidst the chanting of *Jai Shri Guru Maharajji Ki Jai, Jai Shri Swamiji Maharaj-ji Ki Jai* — was taken in a procession. The pyre was erected at the spot predetermined by Swamiji himself, and the monks and devotees laid the body on it. The monks and scores of other persons lit the pyre, and soon it was all ablaze. An intense calm prevailed all around till the flames died out. The next day the monks gathered the sacred relics, some of which were kept at the very spot on which now stands a temple dedicated to Swamiji, and the rest was kept in a copper receptacle shall inspire men everywhere, until the world shall know that it is one with God.' Vision and realisation are imperishable, being of the Truth, they are eternal. The flames of the *Sanatana Dharma* have been rekindled by Ramakrishna-Vivekananda, the duo of the Divine Mother herself, and being *Brahma*'s sun, they have scattered the clouds of

near the altar of Sri Ramakrishna in the main shrine.

The 'splendid symphony of the Universal soul', as Roman Ronald had described Swamiji, stopped playing. The *Math* was absorbed in 'weeping and worship'. There was emptiness all around, but the monks' faith in the Lord soon brought them around, and they were inspired by Swamiji's own words, 'It may be that I shall find it good to get outside my body — to cast it off like a worn-out garment. But I shall not cease to work! I

darkness and ignorance, and bathed the world with the light of the celestial effulgence. The luminous spirits, the founder and the prophet of the new gospel, were truly the Incarnation and a member of His innermost circle of devotees, the *Ishwar-kotis*.

Swami Vivekananda temple at Belur Math.

(opp.) The room at Belur Math where Swamiji entered Mahasamadhi on 4th July 1902.

Glossary of Indian Terms

Aarti	Traditional waving of lamps in worship	Atmano Mokshartam Jagadhitaya Cha	Salvation of the soul for the good of the world/everybody
Acharya	Teacher; Guru		
Adi-Ganga	The mythological, reputedly original, route of the river Ganges	Avatar	Incarnation
		Babu	A word used either before or after a name taken with respect
Adwaita	Non-dual, one which does not have a second; the only one	Bajra	A type of houseboat
Adwaitin	A follower of Adwaita philosophy	Bel	Wood apple
Adwaitism	Monotheism	Bhakta	Devotee
Ahimsa	Non-violence	Bhakti	Devotion; love of God
Akash	Ether	Bhangi	Sweeper, a member of low caste
Alaukik	Of finer matter	Bhikku	Buddhist monk
Amavasya	No moon	Bodhi	Buddha had attained enlightenment under such a tree in Gaya, and it is said that two graftings were done from that same tree, of which the first was planted at Anuradhapuram in Sri Lanka (Ceylon), and a later second one at Sarnath in India
Anna-Satra	Anna=Food, and Satra=Offering; The offering of food		
Apara	Inaugural/Primary, usually associated with Bhakti		
Asana	Small mat used for sitting	Brahma	The God of creation; the Creator
Ashram	Hermitage	Brahmachari	One who practices absolute abstinence
Atman	Soul; self		

Brahmacharini	A female brahmachari	Dwaita	Dualism
Brahmacharya	Absolute abstinence	Ekadoshi	The eleventh day after either the full moon or the new moon, an auspicious day
Brahma-muhurt	The moment of the first light of dawn		
		Fakir	Mohammedan mendicant
Brahman/Brahmin	One belonging to the priestly caste, supposedly highest in the hierarchy	Gauna	Preparatory
		Gerua	Ochre/Saffron colour, the colour of the robes worn by Hindu monks
Buddha Ashtami	An auspicious day for the Buddhists falling on the eighth lunar day after the new moon, usually in the month of February	Ghat	Wharf; jetty; approachable bank of a river used for bathing or even funeral purposes
Bustee	Shantytown	Guru	Spiritual teacher
Chandal	of low caste	Gurukul	An educational system where the student lived with the guru or teacher and learnt inhouse from him
Daan	Giving away in gift		
Danda	Staff	Guru Maharaj	The guru considered as the sovereign
Daridra	Poor	Gyan	Spiritual Knowledge
Darshana	Philosophical outook	Hakim	A Mohammedan doctor
Data	Charitable (person)	Hom	Offerings made in the fire
Devi	A word used either before or after a woman's name showing veneration to her	Hookah	Indian smoking pipe
		Ishwar	God
Dewan	Secretary cum manager of a princely state	Japa	Muttering of prayers; a form of praying with the rosary
Dham	House/residence; also used to denote the abode of God	Janmashtami	The birthday of Lord Krishna which falls on the eighth lunar day after the full moon, usually in the month of August
Dharma	Religion		
Dundies	Sort of palanquins used to carry people on hilly terrains	Ji	A suffix to a name showing respect to the person
Durbar	Princely court	Kaal-Chakra	Wheel of time
Durga Pujo	Worship of the goddess Durga, ritually performed usually in the month of October	Kalpas	Ages; Time Cycle

Kamandalu	Ascetic's water pot		leading the person to the realisation of God
Karma	Action of body or mind, or both	Nistha	Determination
Kaviraj	An Ayurvedic doctor	Pahalwan	Athelete/Wrestler
Khichuri	Gruel made of rice and lintels	Panchvati	Panch=Five, Vat=Tree; Assemblage of five holy trees
Kumari Pujo	Kumari=Virgin, Pujo=Worship; The worship of a girl child representing the values of purity, and thus considered the Mother of the Universe	Para	Highest form, usually used in conjunction with Bhakti, wherein suffering is overcome by giving up useless craving and one realises God in virtually everything
Lathi	A multi-purpose wooden stick used as a walking stick, or even for duels	Patanjali	Highest texts of Raja Yoga
Laukik	Of gross matter	Pathshala	Traditional Indian primary school
Maa	Mother	Peepal tree	Holy fig tree
Maharaja	Sovereign	Pradakshin	Circumambulation
Mahasamadhi	A trance during which the soul of a holy man leaves his body.	Prana	Life
Mantra(s)	The necessary verse(s) required for any/particular ritualistic performance	Pratima	Idol, usually made of clay, used for worshipping
Math	Monastery	Puja/Pujo	Worship
Maya	Illusion	Pundit/Pandit	A learned man
Mlechchha	Outcast	Punya-Kshetra Holy place	Punya=Holy, Kshetra=Place;
Mukti	Emancipation	Puranas	Ancient Hindu Scriptures
Muni	Saint	Rajas	Activity
Munshi	Chief cashier	Ram khadi	A kind of red tinged writing chalk
		Ram rajya	The kingdom of Lord Rama, associated with benevolent governance
Nirvana	Final emancipation of the soul	Rishi	Sage
Nirvikalpa Samadhi	A trance leading to final liberation of the soul through absolue control over one's mind and senses	Sadhu	Holy man

Sahib	A word used before or after a name, or even independently, to denote a man of high stature	Tapasya	Meditation
		Thakore	A title denoting a big landlord or a prince of a small State
Samadhi	Trance		
Samaj	Society	Thakur	God
Samrat	Emperor	Tirath-Yatra/Tirtha	Pilgrimage
Sanatana Dharma	Eternal Religion, another name of Hinduism	Upanishad(s)	Any of the 108 known texts containing the prose and verse of the Vedas
Sanyasi	Wandering monk	Ustad	Expert
Sat-Chi-Anand/ Sachchidanand	Existence-Knowledge- Bliss	Vaishnav	Devotee of Lord Vishnu
		Vaishnavite	Follower of Vaishnav Dharma, a religion for worshipping Lord
Sati	A woman extremely devoted to her husband, and even ready to enter her husband's funeral pyre alive	Vishnu	
		Vakil	A legal practitioner
Satyamev Jayate	In truth there is victory; truth prevails	Vedanta	Conclusion of the Vedas, the Hindu Holy Scriptures
Seth	A wealthy man		
Shaiva	Devotee of Lord Shiva	Vidya	Intellectual Knowledge
Shakta	Worshippers of Shakti in the form of the Divine Mother	Viraj-yagna	Religious offering connected with the initiation into monkhood
Shakti	Strength	Visistha	Distinguished
Shakya Muni	The name by which Buddha is known and worshipped by the Hindus	Yatra	Journey, usually associated with pilgrimage
Shamiana	Canopy	Yoga	Abstract meditation
Shishya	Pupil; Student	Yogodyan	Literally meaning a garden (Udyan) to perform Yoga, it was the name of a garden house of a lay disciple of Sri Ramakrishna
Shiva Lingam	Phallic sculpture symbolic of Lord Shiva and an object of worship		
Siddha-Kshetra	Sanctified place	Zemindar	Landlord of vast areas of land
Sutras	Aphorisms	Zenana	A system wherein women are allowed to come in front of men only when fully clad from head to feet
Syce	Stable groom		
Tamas	Idleness; inertia		